F*CK YES F*CK NO

THE NO F*CKS GIVEN GUIDE TO SAYING NO, SETTING BOUNDARIES, AND LIVING LIFE ON YOUR TERMS

For the ones who are done with overthinking and pleasing everyone but themselves—this book is your brutally honest guide to saying yes to what matters and no to what doesn't.

Disclaimer

This book is not for the faint of heart, the perpetually offended, or anyone who insists on taking life too seriously. It's also not a substitute for professional advice, mental health guidance, or the wisdom of a licensed therapist. If you're dealing with any serious issues that require help beyond what a book can offer, please reach out to a qualified professional.

Fair warning: This book contains sarcasm, blunt language, brutal honesty, and potentially some ideas that may challenge your current way of thinking. The concepts within are designed to help readers rethink where they place their energy, but remember: what you do with this advice is entirely up to you. You are responsible for your own choices, and we're not liable if a newfound "f*ck-free" attitude leads to any unexpected life changes, confrontations, or sudden clarity about things you don't actually want to be doing.

So, read with an open mind, a sense of humor, and maybe a pinch of salt. If you're easily offended or allergic to personal growth, consider this your cue to close the book. For everyone else, welcome aboard, and get ready for a dose of unapologetic self-reflection.

Disclaimer over. Now go give fewer f*cks responsibly.

You Know What This Is

WHY GIVING A F*CK IS OVERRATED

Let's get something straight right off the bat: giving a f*ck about everything is the fastest way to burn out, stress out, and waste your one wild and precious life. Think about it—how often do you find yourself lying awake, replaying moments that, in the grand scheme, are utterly meaningless? A coworker's snide remark, a stranger's online comment, or your aunt's unsolicited life advice. The truth is, we're drowning in opinions, judgments, and all the little worries we've convinced ourselves we *should* care about. Spoiler alert: most of these things don't deserve your energy, let alone your peace of mind.

Caring too much isn't just exhausting; it's like handing over the keys to your happiness to everyone and everything around you. Because, here's the truth: most of what we obsess over doesn't deserve the time, energy, or mental space we give it. The coworker who questioned your outfit, the neighbor who threw a subtle dig about your lawn, even the friend who has a "helpful" critique of your life choices—they're all fleeting blips in your life. You don't owe them a second of your time, but all too often, we act as though we do.

So why do we care? The answer's simple: we've been trained to. Society has us thinking that caring about everything and everyone is somehow noble, as if being constantly concerned with what others think is some sort of high achievement. We're taught to be polite, to fit in, to keep our heads down, and to give far more f*cks than we can afford. But here's the truth nobody tells you—caring about everything and everyone doesn't make you noble; it makes you drained. And it makes you resentful of a life that's slipping by under the weight of everyone else's expectations.

This book is your permission slip to let all that go. It's about learning the art of selective caring. Think of it as managing your "f*ck budget"—you only have so many to give, so why are you wasting them on things that don't make your life better? You wouldn't spend your last dollar on a useless trinket, so why are you blowing your mental energy on things that don't actually serve you?

Here's the great thing about taking control of what you care about: it's like turning on a light switch in a room you didn't know was dark. When you stop giving a f*ck about what everyone thinks, you finally free up space to focus on what *you* think, what *you* value, and what actually brings you joy. It's about reclaiming your attention, and, honestly, your sanity.

Now, I get it—this whole "stop caring" thing isn't an easy switch. For some of us, caring is second nature; we've practically been raised to be concerned with everyone else's feelings and opinions.

It can feel like breaking a habit you didn't even realize you had. That's why we're not going all-or-nothing here. This book is going to walk you through different ways to give fewer f*cks. Think of it as a "choose your own adventure" in freedom. Each chapter will offer both a gentle and a more hardcore approach, so whether you're ready to start with baby steps or make a dramatic leap, you'll find a path that works for you.

If you're looking for light advice on how to ease into not caring, I've got you covered. And if you're ready to torch all unnecessary f*cks with the force of a thousand suns, this book is ready for that too. It's about finding your personal threshold, figuring out what's worth your time and energy, and giving yourself the space to live unapologetically.

Ahead, we're going to dive into practical ways to let go of other people's opinions, manage expectations, and resist the relentless pull to care about things that don't add to your happiness. By the end, you'll have your very own f*ck filter, a toolkit for deciding what truly matters and what you're better off ignoring.

So, if you're ready to break free from the endless cycle of caring too much, you're in the right place. Grab a drink, get comfortable, and let's get real about why caring less is one of the most freeing decisions you can make. Here's the bottom line: when you start being selective about what you care about, you finally create the mental space to actually enjoy your life. Because once you stop giving a f*ck about the noise, you'll finally start living for what matters.

CHAPTER 1

THE F*CK BUDGET

"You can't pour from an empty cup—decide where to spend your fcks wisely."

Welcome to the *Fck Budget. Think of it as your personal ledger for caring—a system that keeps you from overdrafting on all the things that don't serve you. Here's the deal: you only have so many fcks* to give in this life, and they're not an unlimited resource. Every day, you're handing out bits of your energy, your focus, your time—all precious, all finite—and once they're gone, they're gone. So, if you're using them on things that don't genuinely matter, then you're wasting your f*cks like pennies on a scratch-off ticket.

Imagine it this way: if your daily energy is a bank account, then giving a fck is like swiping your debit card. Do it too often, and suddenly, you're bankrupt. Overdraft fees of stress, burnout, and resentment start to pile up. But if you're intentional with each fck, saving them for what truly matters, then guess what? You get to actually *enjoy* your life without feeling like you're being pulled in every direction by things that, deep down, don't mean anything to you.

WHY YOUR F*CK BUDGET MATTERS

Your Fck Budget is about priorities. You don't have to be a people-pleasing martyr, handing out your fcks like flyers on a busy street corner. Here's the cold truth: not everyone and everything deserves your energy. Not every opinion, every trend, every whisper of social expectation is worth your peace of mind. Your time, your mental space, your emotions—these are high-value assets. It's time to start treating them that way.

To get started with your F*ck Budget, you're going to break down where you're currently spending your f*cks and decide if those investments are actually paying off. Spoiler: a lot of them probably aren't. Think of this as doing a full financial audit, but instead of pennies and dollars, we're dealing in pure, unfiltered f*cks.

THE LIGHT APPROACH

If you're just dipping your toes in the waters of not giving a f*ck, don't worry—you don't have to go cold turkey on all your cares. Start small. This approach is about identifying the areas where you can afford to care less, so you can save your energy for the stuff that actually matters. Consider this the "I'll have one slice, not the whole pizza" approach to not giving a f*ck.

1. Strangers' Opinions? Hard Pass.

One of the easiest places to cut back is on the opinions of strangers. People you'll likely never see again, people who scroll by on social media, people who don't know a single thing about you but feel compelled to comment on your life anyway. Here's a pro tip: their opinions are essentially worthless. Whether you impress them or not, these folks will forget about you five minutes later because they're too busy caring about their own lives. So why should their passing thoughts rent space in your head?

2. The Quest for Perfection? Overrated.

Another easy place to trim the fat is your own perfectionism. Stop caring if every project is flawless, if every decision is 100% right, or if you look Instagram-ready every day of your life. Perfection is exhausting, and guess what? No one actually notices if you fall short. Settle for "good enough" in the areas that don't define you—save your high standards for the stuff that counts.

3. The Comparison Game? Delete Your Membership.

Comparison is one of the biggest drains on your F*ck Budget, so it's time to cut ties. Social media makes it all too easy to compare your life to someone else's highlight reel, but here's the truth: other people's lives have nothing to do with you. Their success doesn't mean your failure, and their choices don't invalidate yours. Play your own game, live by your own rules, and remember: their opinions don't determine your worth.

The Heavy Approach

Ready to go all-in? This approach is for those who want to completely overhaul their caring habits. It's about taking a brutally honest look at your life and cutting out anything that doesn't align with your core values. Imagine walking through your life with a red pen and crossing out every obligation, opinion, and expectation that doesn't serve the person you want to be. Extreme? Maybe. Effective? Absolutely.

1. Identify What Actually Matters to *You*

The foundation of this approach is knowing your core values—what matters most to you, regardless of what anyone else thinks. Make a list, a short one, of the top 3–5 things that genuinely drive you. This could be your family, your career, your personal growth, your art, your peace of mind—whatever is most important to *you*. Then, start shaping your life around these priorities and toss everything else out the window. You're building a life that fits *your* vision, not everyone else's.

2. Ruthlessly Edit Your Social Circle

Friends, acquaintances, social commitments—if they don't align with who you are and where you're headed, it's time to let them go. Harsh? Maybe, but it's also liberating. Why waste your limited energy on relationships that don't uplift you? If they drain you, if they don't respect your time, if they're always adding stress to your life, then they don't deserve a place in your F*ck Budget. Focus on the people who genuinely care about you and who inspire you to be your best self.

3. Adopt a "Core-Only" Mentality

From now on, anything that doesn't contribute to your core values or long-term happiness doesn't get a f*ck. Seriously. Treat your attention like VIP access—no one gets in without a ticket. Skip the gossip, the petty arguments, the endless scroll of mindless content. Choose to spend your time and energy only on the things that make you feel alive, grounded, and genuinely fulfilled. It's not about shutting out the world; it's about curating the parts that actually matter.

SPEND YOUR F*CKS LIKE GOLD

Your F*ck Budget is about being intentional with what you care about. Stop letting every minor thing steal your peace of mind. Think of your energy, time, and focus as assets. You wouldn't toss money around without thinking, so why let your mental and emotional currency slip through your fingers on things that don't serve you?

By the end of this chapter, you should have a clearer picture of what really deserves your f*cks—*and what doesn't. Don't be afraid to make some cuts. Trust me, it'll feel like ripping off a band-aid you didn't realize was holding you back. When you take control of your Fck Budget, you're choosing yourself, your values, and your own happiness. And that? That's worth every single f*ck you've got.*

So, grab a pen, get to work on that list, and start being choosy about where you spend your f*cks. Because here's the truth: life's too damn short to care about things that don't matter.

THE F*CK BUDGET TO-DO

Exercises:

1. **Track Your "F*cks" for a Week:** For one week, keep a running tally of things that drain your energy or frustrate you. At the end of each day, write down any situations, people, or tasks that you noticed took a "f*ck" from you.

2. **Create a "Need-to-Care" List:** Make a list of areas where you feel obligated to give a f*ck. For each item, ask, "Is this truly worth my energy?" If not, cross it off and make a commitment to stop investing your time there.

Journal Prompts:

- "Where am I giving too many f*cks, and what's driving me to keep doing it?"
- "What would my life look like if I spent my f*cks only on things that truly matter to me?"

THE SOCIAL F*CK TAX

"The price of fitting in is often too high—choose to stand out, unapologetically."

UNDERSTANDING THE "SOCIAL F*CK TAX"

Alright, it's time to shine a light on a sneaky little thief that's been quietly robbing you of your peace and energy: the Social F*ck Tax. *What's the Social F*ck Tax?* It's the price you pay every time you give your energy to keep up with other people's expectations, judgments, or opinions about how you "should" be living. We're not talking about caring for the people you love or respecting the values that genuinely matter to you—this is about all the *extra* stuff, the silent tax that keeps you in line with what society thinks is "acceptable."

Social expectations are relentless. From how you dress, to the job you choose, to whether you're married or single, to your life goals and beyond, society's got an opinion. The world has built-in rules and subtle pressures to keep you fitting into a box. But here's the deal: society's checklist for "success" is usually more about maintaining the status quo than helping you thrive. It's a silent tax that drains your energy, dims your self-worth, and keeps you living a life that's not even *yours*. But the good news? You can choose to stop paying it. This chapter is your permission slip to start opting out.

THE LIGHT APPROACH

Let's say you're not ready to blow up every social convention in your life just yet. That's cool. This lighter approach is all about learning how to politely, quietly, and confidently decline the opinions that don't serve you. Think of it as setting boundaries without rocking the boat too much—you're easing your way into owning your choices without letting every voice around you influence your peace of mind.

1. Mastering the Art of the Neutral Nod

Here's a simple but powerful tool: the neutral nod. Picture this: someone's sharing their two cents about your life—maybe it's a relative commenting on your career, a friend giving you unsolicited advice about your relationship, or some stranger telling you how you should dress. Instead of reacting, instead of getting defensive, just give them a calm, neutral nod. It's the perfect way to say, "I hear you," without actually agreeing, without engaging, and without letting their opinion settle in your mind.

The neutral nod is your way of acknowledging someone without surrendering your own stance. It lets you engage just enough to be polite while keeping your mental boundaries firmly intact. Try it out next time someone's giving you feedback you didn't ask for—you'll be surprised at how freeing it feels to let their words just bounce off of you. The best part? People often think they've been "heard" and will move on without trying to convince you further.

2. Deflect, Don't Defend

Ever notice how people love to put you on the defensive about your own choices? Someone questions your career move, your taste in clothes, the food on your plate, and suddenly you're explaining yourself as if you're on trial. Here's a game-changer: don't defend. Instead, *deflect.* Instead of launching into an explanation, simply deflect with a light, non-committal response.

Example: when someone says, "Why on earth would you choose *that* job?" just shrug and say, "Because I wanted to." Or try, "It works for me." When someone questions your life choices, a simple, "Hmm, interesting" can end the conversation right there. By deflecting, you're conserving your energy, sidestepping unnecessary debate, and avoiding the exhausting spiral of explaining yourself. Deflection is about protecting your peace.

3. Choose Your Allies Wisely

Here's the thing: not everyone's opinion deserves space in your mind. There are a few people in life whose opinions genuinely matter—the friends, family, or mentors who have your best interest at heart, who know the real you, and who offer guidance from a place of love. These are the people you want in your corner because they'll support you *even when* they don't understand every choice you make. They're the ones who get it, who respect your journey, and who don't need you to fit a mold.

Instead of trying to satisfy everyone, focus on satisfying these few. Let them be your sounding board, your sanity check. The more you choose whose opinions actually matter, the more you'll realize how little the rest of the world's judgment really means. And with your mental space free from everyone else's noise, you'll have more room to grow into the person *you* want to be.

The Heavy Approach

If you're ready to go all-in, this approach is for those who are done letting society's rulebook dictate their lives. Breaking free from conventional validation means you're not just skirting around unwanted opinions—you're tearing down the entire framework of social expectations and building your own rules from scratch. It's about living for *your* values, *your* dreams, and *your* definition of success.

1. Define Your Own Success

Let's get one thing clear: society's definition of success is one-size-fits-all, and it's way too small for most of us. The classic path—career, marriage, mortgage, kids, retirement—is just one version. And guess what? If it doesn't fit who you are, you have every right to redefine it.

Take a moment to sit down and make a list of what truly matters to you. Forget about what society says. Maybe freedom matters to you, or maybe creativity, adventure, or personal growth is what drives you. Write down what *your* dream life looks like, even if it doesn't match what others expect. From now on, this is your compass. Any goal, obligation, or expectation that doesn't align with this personal vision? It's time to let it go. You're not here to live someone else's version of "success"; you're here to define and live your own.

2. Embrace the "So What?" Mindset

If you're going to challenge the rules, you're going to need a new mantra. Here it is: *So what?* This little phrase is your ultimate tool for dismantling unnecessary validation. When someone questions your life choices or society throws a "should" your way, take a deep breath and think, *So what?* So what if I'm not following the traditional path? So what if people don't get it? So what if my life doesn't fit the mold?

Asking "So what?" takes the sting out of social pressure. It's a reminder that your life doesn't need to make sense to anyone else. The only thing that matters is that it makes sense to *you.* Each time you face judgment or skepticism, use this phrase as a shield to deflect their expectations. The "So What?" mindset is about radical self-acceptance—it's choosing to believe that your worth isn't tied to anyone's approval.

3. Make Peace with Being Misunderstood

Living authentically means, inevitably, some people just won't get it. You might be misunderstood, labeled "weird" or "selfish," or criticized for going against the grain. This fear of being misunderstood keeps a lot of people paying the Social F*ck Tax their entire lives. But here's a game-changer: make peace with it. Accept that not everyone will understand your journey, and let that be *okay.*

When you're living in alignment with your own truth, you don't need the world's validation. Understand this: people misunderstand things that challenge their own beliefs or make them uncomfortable. That's their issue, not yours. So the next time you feel pressured to explain yourself, remember that living authentically doesn't require a permission slip. Let them misunderstand you, and go about your life knowing that it's none of their business anyway.

Ditching the Social F*ck Tax for Good

The Social F*ck Tax is a toll on your mind and spirit that you don't have to keep paying. It's the cost of living up to expectations that don't serve you, aligning yourself with opinions that don't resonate, and sacrificing your peace for validation that doesn't fulfill you. But here's the power move: you can opt out.

Start small if you need to—use the light approach to set boundaries, deflect unwanted opinions, and keep your mental space clear. And if you're ready to go all-in, redefine success for yourself, embrace the "So What?" mindset, and make peace with being misunderstood. Once you stop investing in other people's opinions, you'll be shocked at how much lighter, freer, and more *yourself* you feel.

Life is too short to live on anyone else's terms. Drop the Social F*ck Tax, keep your peace, and start building a life that's fully, unapologetically *yours.*

THE "SOCIAL F*CK TAX" TO-DO

Exercises:

1. **Say "No" Once This Week:** *This week, practice saying "no" to one invitation, task, or favor that feels more like a social obligation than a genuine desire.*

2. **Drama Detox Challenge:** *Identify one source of drama or gossip in your life (a friend, coworker, or even a social media account) and limit your interaction with it for a week.*

Journal Prompts:

- *"Where am I paying a 'Social F*ck Tax' by caring too much about others' expectations?"*

-

CHAPTER 3

PRO CRITICISM HANDLER

"Criticism says more about the critic than it does about you—take it or leave it, but don't own it."

Let's talk about criticism. It's that lovely little cocktail of other people's opinions, insecurities, and judgments all shaken up and poured onto your life—usually without an invitation. Criticism is everywhere. It's in your inbox, on your social media feed, coming from your family dinner table, sometimes even lurking in the casual comments of your friends. People love to tell you what you're doing wrong, how you could be better, or why you're somehow "missing the mark." But here's the question: why does it sting so much? Why does it feel like a personal attack, even when it's wrapped up as "constructive feedback"?

The truth is, criticism says a lot more about the person dishing it out than the person receiving it. Often, criticism isn't even about you; it's about them—their own insecurities, doubts, and unmet needs. Think about it: when was the last time you felt totally happy and fulfilled and then thought, Hey, you know what would make me feel even better? Telling someone else how they could improve! Probably never. People criticize because it makes them feel in control or, quite frankly, because they're projecting their own issues onto you. Knowing this is key to handling criticism like a pro, because once you realize criticism is often a reflection of someone else's baggage, you'll stop carrying it around yourself.

This chapter is all about developing your criticism radar and learning how to deflect the opinions that don't serve you. We'll start with a gentle approach for those who want to ease into it and move to a full-on "deflective shield" for those ready to become virtually bulletproof.

Why Criticism Is Usually About Them, Not You

Let's break it down: most criticism is someone else's attempt to control, deflect, or deal with their own insecurities. Maybe they see something in you that reminds them of what they haven't achieved, so they nitpick your progress. Or they feel insecure about a choice they didn't make, so they criticize you for making it. Other times, people criticize just because they feel uncomfortable with anything that challenges their own comfort zone. If you're going for something they never had the courage to do, they might tear you down just to protect their own ego.

Criticism is rarely a straightforward assessment. It's usually wrapped in layers of bias, fear, jealousy, or unprocessed issues. Knowing this lets you take each critique with a heavy dose of skepticism. Next time someone throws a "helpful" suggestion or pointed comment your way, try asking yourself, What does this really say about them? More often than not, the criticism reveals their values, their fears, or their need to control, not some undeniable truth about you.

THE LIGHT APPROACH

Maybe you're not ready to outright ignore every piece of feedback that comes your way. That's fine—there's a way to handle criticism without letting it invade your peace. We call this the "Listen and Release" approach. It's about hearing the feedback, filtering out anything useful, and then letting the rest slide right off you like water on a duck's back. Here's how it works.

1. Pause, Don't Pounce

First, when someone criticizes you, take a breath. Don't jump to defend yourself, explain, or counter-argue right away. Criticism has a way of pushing our buttons, so give yourself a moment to pause before responding. By pausing, you're creating mental space to ask yourself, Does this really matter to me? Often, you'll find that it doesn't. The pause keeps you from reacting emotionally, which is a powerful first step in handling criticism with grace.

2. Separate the Message from the Messenger

Once you've paused, try to separate the actual feedback from the person giving it. Is there any value in what they're saying, or is it all wrapped up in their own issues? Maybe your boss suggests you be more organized—not a terrible piece of advice. But if your notoriously disorganized friend tells you the same thing, you might want to take it with a grain of salt. Evaluate the criticism for what it is, rather than letting the person delivering it dictate its importance.

3. Ask, "Is This Useful?"

This is the magic question. Not all criticism is bad—sometimes, feedback is genuinely useful. But useful criticism is constructive, clear, and given with respect, not meant to tear you down. After you've taken a breath and evaluated the source, ask yourself, Is this useful? If the answer is yes, take it as an opportunity to learn or grow. But if it's just noise, let it go. Picture yourself letting their words drift away, like leaves in a river. You don't need to carry every single critique along with you.

4. Release with a Mental "Thank You, Next"

Once you've extracted anything helpful, it's time to release the rest. Mentally thank the person for their "feedback," smile, nod, and move on. Picture it like a "Thank you, next" in your head—a polite acknowledgment that doesn't mean you're taking their words to heart. This subtle practice lets you engage politely without getting pulled into their narrative or taking on criticism that doesn't belong to you.

THE HEAVY APPROACH

Ready to go hard-core? The heavy approach is for those who are done letting other people's insecurities, judgments, and unsolicited advice invade their mental space. This approach is about developing a "deflective shield," a near-impenetrable barrier that protects you from all criticism that doesn't serve your personal growth. This isn't just about ignoring feedback; it's about mastering the art of selective hearing and keeping your peace untouchable.

1. Adopt a "Selective Listening" Mindset

Selective listening is about choosing which voices deserve your attention and which don't. Imagine you have an invisible remote control with a mute button that lets you tune out any criticism that doesn't serve you. From now on, you're only listening to feedback that's constructive, relevant, and aligned with your goals. Everything else? Muted. Picture yourself turning down the volume on the critical voices, silencing them so that they fade into background noise.

When you adopt this mindset, you start to realize how much criticism is just chatter. Not every voice has wisdom to offer, so why waste your time listening to them all? By filtering out the noise, you free up energy for your own goals and values.

2. Create a Mental "Bouncer"

Picture a bouncer standing guard at the entrance of your mind. Every piece of feedback is like a guest trying to get in, and the bouncer is there to decide who makes the cut. The rule is simple: if the criticism isn't constructive, respectful, or relevant to your goals, it doesn't get past the door.

Imagine someone criticizes you, but instead of letting their words sink in, your mental bouncer stops them cold. The bouncer takes one look at that criticism, says, "Sorry, you're not on the list," and keeps it out. Only the feedback that helps you grow and aligns with your values gets in. Everything else? Blocked.

3. Practice the "Mirror Deflection" Technique

Here's a powerful visualization: every time someone throws a criticism at you, picture a mirror in front of you that reflects it right back. Their words bounce off the mirror and head straight back to where they came from. This technique is about reminding yourself that their criticism is a reflection of them, not you.

Picture someone telling you, "I don't think you're good enough for that job," and imagine those words hitting the mirror and bouncing back to them. Their criticism can't affect you if it never makes it past the mirror. This technique allows you to stay calm, grounded, and unaffected by other people's negative projections.

4. Embrace the "Unbothered Mindset"

The final step in handling criticism like a pro is fully embracing an "unbothered" mindset. This isn't about pretending not to care—it's about genuinely choosing not to care. The unbothered mindset says, "I'm too focused on my own growth and goals to waste my time on irrelevant opinions." It's a form of radical self-confidence that allows you to stay on your path without letting anyone else's commentary throw you off course.

With this mindset, you start to see criticism as just background noise—like static on an old radio. It's there, but it doesn't interfere with your main broadcast. Embracing the unbothered mindset is about trusting yourself so completely that other people's judgments lose their power.

Own Your Peace, Filter the Noise

Criticism is an inevitable part of life, but you get to decide whether it builds you up or weighs you down. By understanding that most criticism stems from other people's insecurities, you can start viewing it with a healthy dose of skepticism. The light approach—listening and releasing—gives you a way to handle criticism politely without absorbing it. And the heavy approach—developing a deflective shield—allows you to fully own your peace by filtering out all feedback that doesn't serve your growth.

At the end of the day, handling criticism like a pro is about learning to prioritize yourself. It's about knowing that you don't owe anyone your attention, your energy, or your mental space. You get to decide what you let in and what you ignore. So, the next time someone comes at you with a critique, take a breath, ask if it's worth your energy, and, if not, let it bounce off your deflective shield and go right back to where it came from.

*Because life's too short to give a f*ck about criticism that doesn't help you grow.*

Handle Criticism Like a Pro To-Do

Exercises:

1. ***Sort Feedback into "Useful" vs. "Useless":*** *Over the next week, every time you receive feedback or criticism, mentally sort it into one of two categories: useful or useless. Only keep and reflect on the useful stuff.*

2. ***The "Thank You, Next" Practice:*** *When someone offers unhelpful or unsolicited criticism, mentally say, "Thank you, next," and let it go. Practice this for small interactions throughout the week.*

Journal Prompts:

- *"How does criticism usually affect me, and what's the first thing I could change about my response?"*
- *"What would change if I only took criticism from people I trust and respect?"*

CHAPTER 4

EMBRACING IMPERFECTION

"Perfection is a myth—authenticity is your superpower."

Here's the deal: perfection is a myth. It's a cruel trick society plays on us, constantly pushing us to be flawless, to be *better* than everyone else, to have it all together all the time. But here's the thing: no one has it all together. Not even the people who seem like they do. Perfection is like chasing a unicorn—it's a beautiful idea, but it doesn't exist. So why are we all still desperately trying to catch it?

This chapter is your wake-up call to stop pretending you have it all figured out and to embrace the *real* you—flaws, mistakes, and all. Here's the secret: there's freedom in imperfection. When you stop chasing an impossible ideal and start accepting yourself as you are—messy, imperfect, and gloriously human—you get to live a life that's a hell of a lot more fun. So, let's dive in.

WHY PERFECTION IS OVERRATED (AND COMPLETELY UNATTAINABLE)

Let's get this straight: perfection is a fantasy, a made-up standard that only makes us feel like we're never good enough. We all see the perfectly curated lives online—the flawless selfies, the perfectly decorated homes, the flawless workout routines—and we think, Oh, if I could just get my life together like that, everything would be perfect. But here's the secret—no one's life is perfect. Not even the Instagram influencers whose entire job revolves around creating the illusion of perfection.

The truth is, perfection is subjective. What's "perfect" for one person might be completely wrong for another. So why are we all killing ourselves trying to meet someone else's version of "perfect" when we could be just, well, ourselves? Perfection is exhausting. It's a straight-up energy suck that leaves you constantly chasing after a finish line that doesn't even exist. And guess what? No one notices if your hair is a little messy, or if your lunch isn't photogenic, or if you're 10 minutes late. They're too busy worrying about their own damn lives.

So, here's your permission slip to drop the perfection act. Embrace the fact that you're human. And being human means you're gonna screw up. You're gonna make mistakes. You're gonna say the wrong thing at the wrong time. You're gonna have a bad hair day, eat that extra slice of pizza, and forget to reply to a text message for 48 hours. And guess what? That's okay. That's life.

THE LIGHT APPROACH

Now, if you're the type of person who's been convinced that every little mistake you make is a personal failure, then it's time to dial it down. This approach is about learning to let go of the urge to self-punish every time you mess up. It's about giving yourself permission to be *imperfect* without turning it into a full-on emotional meltdown.

1. Mistakes Are Not the End of the World

First things first: you're going to make mistakes. It's inevitable. You'll miss the deadline. You'll put your foot in your mouth in a conversation. You'll spill coffee on your shirt right before an important meeting. Guess what? It's not the end of the world. Most people won't even remember by tomorrow. So why are you torturing yourself over it for days, replaying the moment in your head like it's the end of your career?

Take a deep breath. Say, *So what?* Mistakes are part of life. They're not a reflection of your worth. So the next time you mess up, stop the negative spiral before it starts. Catch yourself thinking, *Oh no, I'm an idiot,* and switch gears. Remind yourself: mistakes are lessons, not failures. What's the worst that could happen? You move on, you learn from it, and you're better for it. And let's be honest: you'll have a hilarious story to tell later.

2. Don't Beat Yourself Up Over Small Stuff

This one's key: stop beating yourself up for every little thing. You dropped your phone in the toilet? Fine, it happens. You burned your dinner? Great, now you've got an excuse to order pizza. It's the small stuff that often causes the most stress, and if you keep hyper-focusing on every tiny mistake, you'll never get anything done.

Instead of mentally flogging yourself over the "failure," ask yourself: *What's the worst that happens here?* Will anyone even care that you took a longer-than-expected nap instead of finishing your to-do list? Probably not. Will you remember that you wore mismatched socks to work last week? No. It's just a blip in the larger story of your life. So, cut yourself some slack.

3. Laugh at Yourself (Seriously)

A huge part of letting go of perfection is learning to laugh at yourself. Life is funny. Your awkward moments are hilarious. Your embarrassing slip-ups are more relatable than you realize. The next time you mess up, laugh. Really, truly laugh. The more you laugh at your own mistakes, the less power they have over you.

You stop taking yourself so seriously, and suddenly, the pressure lifts.

Being able to laugh at yourself is a game-changer. It's an instant mood booster and a reminder that life is short and ridiculous. The more you can laugh at your own flaws, the less room there is for shame or embarrassment.

The Heavy Approach

Ready to go all-in on authenticity? The heavy approach is all about fully embracing your quirks, flaws, and imperfections—and not just quietly accepting them, but *celebrating* them. This is where you stop hiding who you really are and start showing up unapologetically in all your messy, glorious, real-human glory.

1. Be Proud of Your Weirdness

Listen up: everyone's weird in their own way. Some of us are a little quirky, some of us are awkward as hell, and some of us have a weird obsession with true crime documentaries. Guess what? That's what makes you *you*. And that's amazing. Stop hiding it. The more you embrace the things that make you unique, the more you'll stand out in a world full of people trying to blend in.

Own your weirdness. Celebrate it. If you're a little eccentric, show it off. If you're bad at small talk, own it and say, *I'm not great at this, but I'm working on it.* People love authenticity. The more real you are, the more people will respect you. Plus, being yourself makes life way more fun. It's exhausting pretending to be something you're not. So, throw the "perfect version" of yourself out the window, and let your true colors shine. You're not a carbon copy of someone else—you're a limited edition. Wear that with pride.

2. Share Your Flaws—And Celebrate Them

Here's where we go next-level: start *celebrating* your flaws. I know, it sounds ridiculous, but stay with me. We all have imperfections. Maybe you're the person who's always 10 minutes late to every event (guilty). Or maybe you're a serial over-thinker who can't stop analyzing every conversation. Instead of pretending these things don't exist, just own them. Laugh about them.

Tell your friends, "Yep, I'm always late. I'm working on it. But honestly, I just like to make an entrance." Or, "I overthink everything. And yes, I'm a walking anxiety attack, but I've learned to laugh about it." Owning your flaws doesn't make you weak—it makes you relatable, approachable, and, most importantly, *human.* When you embrace your imperfections, you stop hiding behind a façade and start living in your truth.

3. Stop Apologizing for Being Yourself

Why do we apologize for existing? "Oh, sorry I'm late." "Sorry, I'm just really tired today." "Sorry, I'm a little weird." Stop apologizing for being yourself! Seriously. People will like you more if you stop apologizing for things that don't need an apology. You're not perfect, and that's awesome. So stop pretending to be. Own your quirks, your odd habits, and your imperfections like they're the coolest thing about you. They are.

And if someone doesn't like it? Too bad. They're probably too busy trying to keep up their own mask of perfection. Let them. You're over here living your life unapologetically.

IMPERFECTION IS FREEDOM

Here's the thing: embracing imperfection isn't just about cutting yourself some slack—it's about stepping into your authenticity with both feet. It's about saying, *I'm imperfect, and that's great.* Because in imperfection, there's freedom. There's liberation in being real, in accepting yourself as you are, flaws and all. The more you let go of the need to be perfect, the more room you make for joy, creativity, and actual living.

So, stop beating yourself up for not having it all together. Stop hiding your quirks. Stop pretending to be someone you're not. Be real. Be messy. Be unapologetically you. Because that's the version of yourself that's going to attract the right people, create the best opportunities, and, most importantly, *live a life that's actually worth living.*

Perfection is overrated. Imperfection? That's where the magic happens.

EMBRACING IMPERFECTION TO-DO

Exercises:

1. **Share a "Flaw" or Quirk:** *This week, share one of your quirks or imperfections with someone, no apologies. Whether it's laughing too loud or being a terrible cook, own it and notice how it feels.*

2. **Do One Thing Without Trying to Be Perfect:** *Pick one task this week—writing an email, cooking a meal, or even*

getting dressed—and do it without aiming for perfection. Just let it be "good enough."

Journal Prompts:

- *"What imperfections do I struggle to accept, and why?"*
- *"How would my life be different if I embraced my quirks and flaws fully?"*

CHAPTER 5

DECLINING INVITES

"Saying 'no' isn't rejection; it's a commitment to your peace."

Alright, buckle up because we're about to tackle something that makes a lot of people squirm: saying "no." Not just saying "no" to social events, but also saying "no" to opinions, expectations, and all the unsolicited advice people throw your way. We live in a society that treats "no" like it's a dirty word. It's as if declining something makes you selfish, rude, or ungrateful. Spoiler alert: it doesn't. In fact, "no" is one of the most powerful words in your arsenal. It's a magic little shield that protects your time, energy, and sanity from getting sucked into things you don't want or need.

This chapter is all about saying "no" without guilt and learning how to avoid people-pleasing, so you're not constantly sacrificing your own peace to make everyone else happy. We'll start with the light approach for those of you who are a bit hesitant to say "no" and work our way up to the unapologetic, no-justifications-needed approach for those who are ready to embrace "no" as a lifestyle.

Why Saying "No" Is Actually a Form of Self-Respect

Before we get into the how-to, let's clear up why saying "no" is important. Saying "no" isn't about shutting people out or being cold; it's about self-respect. Every time you say "yes" to something you don't want to do, you're essentially saying "no" to yourself. You're telling yourself that everyone else's needs, opinions, and expectations come before your own. Think about that. Think about how many times you've said "yes" to things you didn't want to do, just to keep the peace, be "nice," or avoid disappointing someone.

But here's the truth: you're allowed to say "no." In fact, you *should* say "no" to things that drain you or don't align with your priorities. Every "no" you say to things that don't serve you is a "yes" to the things that actually matter. And the more you practice saying it, the more you'll start to see "no" as an act of self-respect rather than an act of rebellion. It's like reclaiming a little piece of your own life, one "no" at a time.

THE LIGHT APPROACH

So, maybe you're not ready to start dropping hard "no" bombs on everyone just yet, and that's totally fine. There's a way to say "no" without guilt and without coming off as harsh or cold. This light approach is about politely declining and setting boundaries in a way that's kind, clear, and—most importantly—respectful to yourself.

1. The "Soft No" Approach

Here's a little trick: the "soft no." This is where you politely decline while offering a vague reason that isn't too specific. Let's say someone invites you to a party, but you'd rather binge-watch your favorite show on the couch. Instead of saying, "I'd rather stay home and not talk to anyone," you can say, "Thanks so much for the invite! I'm going to have to pass this time, but I appreciate it." Notice the wording here—there's no long-winded explanation, just a polite decline.

The "soft no" is effective because it gets the message across without you feeling like you're rejecting someone outright. It's a kind way to bow out without sacrificing your own comfort. Use it when you want to say "no" but don't feel like getting into the weeds of *why* you're saying it.

2. The "I'm Taking Time for Myself" Excuse

This one's a gem for declining invitations without guilt. People can get weirdly pushy about why you're not available, so having a go-to reason can be helpful. Next time someone invites you to something that you don't want to attend, say, "I've been really needing some time to recharge, so I'm going to have to pass."

The beauty of this approach is that most people can relate to the need for downtime, so they're less likely to push back. And if they do push back? That's their issue, not yours. You don't owe anyone an explanation beyond, "I'm taking care of myself." Period. This isn't just a way to decline an invite; it's also a great way to remind yourself that it's okay to prioritize your own needs.

3. The Boundary Setting Statement

Sometimes, declining invitations isn't enough—you need to set a boundary to make sure people understand your limits. This one's for the persistent folks in your life who just won't take "no" for an answer. If someone is constantly trying to rope you into things, it's time for a boundary-setting statement like, "I have a lot on my plate right now, so I'm saying 'no' to extra commitments for the time being."

Boundaries aren't about pushing people away; they're about protecting your peace. If someone doesn't respect that, they're showing you exactly why your boundary is necessary. And here's the key: don't apologize for setting boundaries. You don't owe anyone your time or energy unless *you* decide it's worth it.

THE HEAVY APPROACH

Ready to take things to the next level? Here's where we dive into the art of saying "no" with no apologies, no explanations, and absolutely zero guilt. This approach is about reclaiming your right to choose how you spend your time and energy, without feeling like you need to justify yourself.

1. Just Say "No"

No need to wrap it up in niceties. No need for a big, fluffy explanation. If someone invites you to do something and you don't want to go, simply say, "No, thanks." That's it. You don't have to add a reason or an apology. People might be taken aback by your directness, but that's their problem, not yours.

When you say a simple, direct "no," you're showing people that you respect your own boundaries and don't need to sugarcoat it. Think of this as a power move. You're not giving them a foot in the door to negotiate your "no" into a "maybe" or a "yes." You're being clear, honest, and, let's face it, pretty badass. This approach is about owning your decision without feeling like you owe anyone an explanation.

2. Don't Offer a Reason Unless You Want To

The world has conditioned us to believe that saying "no" isn't enough—we're supposed to have a valid, ironclad reason. But here's the reality: *you don't need a reason.* "No" is a complete sentence. The more you explain, the more you open the door for people to argue with your decision, try to guilt-trip you, or find a workaround. So, next time someone asks you why you're not coming to an event, just say, "I'm not able to make it." If they ask why? Politely smile and change the subject.

The less you explain, the stronger your boundary becomes. You're showing them that your "no" stands on its own and doesn't require their approval. Remember: *you don't owe anyone your time, and you certainly don't owe anyone an explanation for how you choose to spend it.*

3. Master the "No, Thanks, But I'm Good" Response

This approach is perfect for declining unwanted opinions as well as invitations. Let's say someone starts giving you advice you didn't ask for—maybe it's about your career, your relationship, or your lifestyle choices. Instead of nodding along and pretending to care, just say, "No, thanks, but I'm good." It's a clear message that you're not interested, and it's a polite way to shut down unwanted advice without being rude.

This one works wonders in shutting down conversations you don't want to engage in. When you use a simple, no-nonsense response like this, you're telling people that you're confident in your choices and don't need their input. It's a way of drawing a line without getting into a debate or having to explain yourself.

4. Embrace the Power of Silence

Here's a pro tip: sometimes, the best response is *no response at all.* If someone's being pushy, overstepping, or just plain not respecting your "no," silence can be your greatest ally. Don't feel obligated to fill every awkward pause with an explanation. If they keep pushing, just smile, say, "I've already given you my answer," and let the silence hang in the air.

Silence can be incredibly powerful because it makes people realize they're not going to get any further with you. They'll either have to accept your decision or sit in the discomfort of their own pushiness. And here's the best part: you don't have to do a thing. Just stay calm, grounded, and confident in your "no."

Saying "No" Without Guilt Is a Superpower

Learning to say "no" is one of the most empowering things you can do for yourself. Every time you say "no" to something that doesn't serve you, you're reclaiming a little piece of your life. You're saying, *My time and energy are valuable, and I'm going to spend them wisely.* Whether you're politely declining with a gentle excuse or unapologetically shutting down a conversation with a simple "no," remember: you have the right to choose where you invest yourself.

At the end of the day, saying "no" isn't selfish. It's self-respect. It's about protecting your peace, prioritizing what matters, and refusing to be a people-pleasing pushover. The next time someone tries to push an invite or an opinion your way, take a deep breath, remind yourself that "no" is a complete sentence, and stand firm. You don't owe anyone your time, energy, or a detailed explanation. So go ahead, say "no" without guilt, and let yourself feel the freedom that comes with living life on *your* terms.

DECLINING INVITES TO-DO

Exercises:

1. ***Say "No" Without Apology or Explanation:*** *Choose one opportunity this week to say "no" without feeling the need to apologize or explain. See how it feels to leave it at, "No, thanks."*

2. ***Social Circle Audit:*** *Make a list of the people who regularly ask things of you or expect you to show up. Reflect on which people are worth saying "yes" to and who might need more boundaries.*

Journal Prompts:

- *"How often do I say 'yes' out of obligation, and how does it make me feel?"*
- *"If I could stop people-pleasing entirely, how would I handle invitations differently?"*

CHAPTER 6
OVERCOMING FOMO

"You're not missing out, you're gaining focus on what really matters."

Let's face it: FOMO is a modern-day epidemic. It's that nagging feeling that if you don't say "yes" to every event, every hangout, every trendy experience, you're somehow missing out on life. We scroll through social media, seeing everyone's "highlight reel" of parties, vacations, and #livingmybestlife selfies, and we start to feel like if we're not constantly out there doing *something*, we're somehow failing. But here's the cold, hard truth: most of those people are just as bored, stressed, and overwhelmed as you are—they're just better at curating it. Real life isn't a 24/7 party, and you're not missing out on anything essential by skipping yet another brunch.

This chapter is about breaking free from the FOMO trap and learning the power of choosing solitude and inner peace over the never-ending hamster wheel of external validation. We're talking about stepping away from the constant noise of other people's lives and focusing on *your own*, building a sense of contentment that isn't dependent on being "in the know" or keeping up with anyone else.

The beauty of overcoming FOMO isn't just that you get your time back; it's that you stop living for everyone else's approval. Imagine waking up and realizing that you don't actually need to be everywhere, know everything, or be included in every invite.

Imagine feeling genuinely happy, even if everyone else is off doing their thing without you. Sound nice? Let's get into it.

WHY FOMO IS JUST A FANCY NAME FOR PEOPLE-PLEASING

At its core, FOMO is about people-pleasing. It's the fear that if you're not constantly "in the mix," people will forget about you, or worse, that you'll somehow be "less cool." It's as if skipping one party will make you invisible. But here's the reality: true confidence isn't about being included; it's about being comfortable with yourself, even if you're alone on a Friday night with a book and a cup of tea. FOMO is just a new twist on an old problem—living for other people's approval.

If you're constantly saying "yes" because you're afraid of missing out, you're letting everyone else dictate how you spend your time and energy. You're handing over control to whoever happens to invite you to the next event. Real freedom comes from making *your own choices*, not letting FOMO drag you around like a leash. And here's the kicker: you can't find inner peace until you break free from the grip of FOMO. It's impossible to be truly content when you're constantly worried about being somewhere else, doing something else, with someone else.

THE LIGHT APPROACH

If you're new to breaking free from FOMO, don't worry—you don't have to go cold turkey. This light approach is all about practicing the art of choosing yourself over social pressure in small, manageable doses. It's about learning to say "no" here and there, just enough to get a taste of how good it feels to prioritize yourself over what everyone else is doing.

1. Skip One Thing, Just to See What Happens

Here's a fun experiment: the next time you get invited to something that you *kind of* want to go to but aren't fully excited about, say "no." Seriously, just say, "Thanks, but I'm going to sit this one out." You don't need a reason. Just decline, and then do *whatever you want instead.* Watch your favorite show, read a book, go for a walk, or just sit in silence—anything but scrolling through social media to see what everyone else is doing.

Notice how it feels. At first, you might feel that pang of "Oh no, am I missing out?" But give it time. Soon, you'll start to realize that nothing catastrophic happens when you skip a single event. The world keeps turning, people go on with their lives, and you get to enjoy a peaceful evening on your own terms.

2. Practice the "Would I Rather?" Test

This little mental trick will save you from saying "yes" to things you don't actually want to do. Next time you're deciding whether to go out, ask yourself, "Would I rather do this *or* would I rather have a night to myself?" If the idea of being alone sounds genuinely better, then skip the event. When you frame it this way, you're making a choice between two things that benefit *you* instead of letting the social pressure make the choice for you.

This test works because it reframes FOMO as a choice between socializing and self-care. Instead of automatically choosing the option that keeps you "in the loop," you're choosing the option that serves your peace of mind. The "Would I Rather?" test reminds you that your happiness doesn't depend on attending every single thing.

3. Challenge Yourself to Enjoy Your Own Company

This might sound basic, but for a lot of people, being alone without distractions is terrifying. If you want to truly overcome FOMO, you need to learn how to actually *like* spending time with yourself.

Challenge yourself to spend an evening alone, doing something you genuinely enjoy, and resist the urge to check your phone or see what everyone else is up to.

When you can sit with yourself, without needing constant stimulation or external validation, you start to build a level of self-confidence that makes FOMO irrelevant. You become someone who's content on their own, which is way more powerful than being someone who always needs to be "in the know."

THE HEAVY APPROACH

Ready to go hardcore? Let's take this up a notch. The heavy approach to beating FOMO is about creating a life that's *intentionally* free of unnecessary noise. This means embracing a minimalist approach to relationships, events, and obligations. You're not just skipping a few social events; you're redesigning your entire social life to reflect what *actually* matters to you.

1. Ruthlessly Edit Your Social Calendar

It's time to take a hard look at your calendar and start cutting. Are there regular events, commitments, or meet-ups that don't genuinely excite you? Are you saying "yes" to people and gatherings that leave you feeling drained rather than fulfilled? If so, it's time to declutter. Look at your social obligations the way you'd look at a closet overflowing with stuff you don't wear—if it doesn't bring you joy, it's gotta go.

Start by identifying the social interactions that *truly* add value to your life. Maybe it's dinner with your closest friends or a monthly book club you genuinely enjoy. Keep those. Everything else? Politely decline, and start saying "no" to any new invites that don't align with your values. A minimalist social calendar isn't about isolating yourself; it's about protecting your time and energy for the things that actually make you happy.

2. Surround Yourself with "Quality Over Quantity" People

When you're intentional about who you spend time with, FOMO becomes less of an issue. Instead of spreading yourself thin across dozens of superficial relationships, focus on a smaller circle of people who genuinely enrich your life. These are the friends who support you, who respect your boundaries, and who make you feel valued.

Once you surround yourself with people who respect your choice to skip an event, FOMO starts to fade away. You'll find that the people who matter don't pressure you, and the people who pressure you don't really matter. By choosing quality over quantity in your relationships, you're creating a support system that doesn't hinge on constant social appearances.

3. Practice the Art of "Joyful Missing Out" (JOMO)

"JOMO" is the opposite of FOMO. It stands for the *Joy of Missing Out,* and it's about actively choosing to skip things and feeling *good* about it. When you embrace JOMO, you're not just sitting out because you're tired or because you need a night off; you're choosing to miss things because you're genuinely happier doing your own thing.

Next time you see people posting about the party, the vacation, or the trendy new event, take a moment to consciously enjoy whatever *you're* doing instead. Maybe you're curled up with a book, taking a long bath, or binging your favorite show. Instead of feeling left out, let yourself feel a deep sense of contentment. You're not "missing out"—you're prioritizing your own happiness. When you make JOMO a habit, you start to crave that peaceful, self-focused time over the chaos of constantly being "in the know."

4. Build a Life You Don't Need a Break From

Here's the ultimate goal of overcoming FOMO: building a life you genuinely love so much that you don't feel like you're missing out on anything. Instead of looking at other people's lives and feeling like you're missing something, create a life that feels fulfilling from the inside out. This doesn't mean every day has to be magical or Instagram-worthy. It just means designing a life where your daily routines, relationships, and environment make you feel at peace.

When you're truly happy with your own life, you don't feel the need to be everywhere, with everyone, doing everything. You're content. You're fulfilled. And that's what real freedom looks like—being so happy with your own choices that you're not swayed by what everyone else is doing.

Choose Your Own Peace Over FOMO

FOMO is just another way of letting society control your choices. It's a trap, a trick, a guilt trip designed to make you feel like you're "less than" if you're not constantly doing something. But when you choose your own peace, your own priorities, and your own happiness, FOMO becomes irrelevant. You're no longer living for external validation; you're living for yourself.

So, start small if you need to—skip one event, take yourself out for a solo evening, or spend an entire weekend without checking social media. And if you're ready to go big, start designing a minimalist, intentional life where every choice, every relationship, and every commitment aligns with who you really are.

Because here's the truth: you're not missing out on life by skipping every party, every event, or every invite. You're only missing out on life if you keep ignoring your own happiness in favor of everyone else's expectations. Choose yourself, build a life that makes you feel whole, and let everyone else chase their own FOMO. You've got better things to do.

OVERCOMING FOMO TO-DO

Exercises:

1. ***JOMO Weekend Challenge:*** *Plan one weekend where you consciously avoid social media and focus only on doing things you enjoy, alone or with close friends. Experience the Joy of Missing Out.*

2. ***Create a "Would I Rather?" List:*** *Next time you're torn between a social event and something you'd rather do, ask yourself, "Would I rather do this or stay in?" Practice choosing yourself over FOMO.*

Journal Prompts:

- *"What am I afraid of missing out on, and why?"*

- *"How can I prioritize what I genuinely want over the pressure to be everywhere, doing everything?"*

CHAPTER 7
PROTECTING YOUR INNER PEACE

"Guard your peace like your life depends on it—because it does."

Inner peace. Sounds nice, right? That calm, centered feeling where nothing and no one can shake you. But let's be honest: in a world full of drama, gossip, unsolicited opinions, and people who seem determined to stir the pot, finding that inner peace feels like trying to meditate in the middle of a rock concert. The truth is, inner peace doesn't just "happen." You don't magically wake up one day immune to everyone else's nonsense. You have to *protect* it, to actively create a fortress around it, especially if you want to keep your sanity intact in the face of all the world's chaos.

This chapter is about learning how to guard your mental space like it's the most valuable asset you have—because it is. Your inner peace is what allows you to focus, stay calm, and feel happy despite the noise around you. Without it, you're vulnerable to every bit of gossip, every opinion, every ounce of drama that crosses your path. But with it? You're untouchable.

We'll start with some gentle, low-key ways to distance yourself from negativity and work up to the heavy-hitter moves for those ready to go all-in on protecting their peace. Ready to build some walls around your mental sanctuary? Let's get into it.

WHY PROTECTING YOUR PEACE MATTERS

Let's get one thing straight: no one is going to protect your peace for you. There will always be people with opinions about your life, people who thrive on drama, people who think gossip is an Olympic sport. If you let them, these people will chip away at your peace piece by piece, until you're a ball of stress and self-doubt.

Here's the hard truth: protecting your peace is non-negotiable. It's about survival. Your mental space is sacred, and when you let people invade it with their negativity, you're letting them rob you of your happiness, your focus, and your energy. Protecting your peace isn't selfish; it's self-preservation. It's drawing a line that says, "My happiness is not up for grabs."

THE LIGHT APPROACH

If you're not ready to go full fortress mode, that's okay. You don't have to drop all toxic people at once or dramatically cut everyone out of your life. Sometimes, it's enough to create a little distance—just enough space to shield yourself from the worst of the drama and negativity. This approach is about small, subtle moves that keep your peace intact without creating waves.

1. Set Your "Drama Filter" to Low

Think of your mind as a filter, like the one on your social media feed. You have control over what you let through. When people around you start gossiping, judging, or spiraling into drama, mentally set your "drama filter" to low. Imagine their words just passing right over your head. You're there physically, but emotionally? You're miles away. Nod politely, keep your responses neutral, and let the negativity flow right past you without sinking in.

When you start treating drama as background noise, it loses its power. You'll find that you're not as affected by other people's chaos because you're not fully engaging with it. You're a spectator, not a participant. This tiny shift can do wonders for your inner peace.

2. Politely Pivot Out of Gossip

Gossip is one of the biggest threats to inner peace because it drags you into other people's business and fills your mind with unnecessary noise. The next time someone starts a gossip session, try politely pivoting the conversation. Say something like, "I'm not sure about that, but have you heard about…" and redirect to a more positive or neutral topic.

This subtle move lets you avoid the drama without making anyone feel judged. And if they're really insistent on gossiping? That's a red flag. Make a mental note that this is someone who might need to be kept at arm's length if you're serious about protecting your peace.

3. Set Emotional Boundaries

Sometimes, people don't realize they're invading your mental space. They might be used to venting to you about their problems or dumping their emotional baggage without noticing the impact it has on you. This is where gentle boundaries come in. The next time someone starts emotionally unloading on you, say something like, "I care about you, but I've got a lot on my plate right now and need to protect my energy."

This simple boundary doesn't shut them out; it just lets them know you're not their emotional dumping ground. Boundaries are like invisible shields—once you put them up, people learn that your peace is off-limits.

THE HEAVY APPROACH

Alright, now we're stepping it up. This approach is for those who are done with half-measures and ready to go full fortress mode on their inner peace. It's not for the faint-hearted, but it's incredibly effective. Sometimes, gently distancing yourself isn't enough. Sometimes, you need to draw a hard line in the sand and cut ties with people who drain your energy, disrespect your boundaries, and threaten your sanity.

1. Identify the "Energy Vampires"

Let's get real: some people are like human black holes, sucking the life out of you every time you interact. They're the ones who constantly complain, stir up drama, and never respect your boundaries. These are "energy vampires." To protect your peace, you need to identify who these people are. Think about the people in your life who leave you feeling drained after every conversation. The ones who never bring anything positive to the table.

Once you identify them, you can start limiting your interactions. This doesn't have to be a dramatic exit—just a gradual withdrawal. Stop answering their calls immediately, take longer to reply to their texts, and make yourself less available. This slow fade sends a message without you having to directly cut them off.

2. Embrace the "No Explanation" Boundary

Sometimes, you need to set boundaries that are firm, clear, and unyielding. Here's the trick: don't explain yourself. If you're cutting someone off, you don't need to give a reason, a speech, or an apology. Just say, "I need some space to focus on myself right now." If they ask why or push for details, simply repeat, "This is something I need to do for my peace."

Explanations invite arguments, and people who don't respect your boundaries will use any excuse to try to convince you to change your mind. Stand firm, keep it short, and don't give them the opening to argue. This might feel uncomfortable at first, but the more you do it, the easier it gets. Remember, you're protecting your peace, not negotiating a peace treaty.

3. Set "Access Levels" for People in Your Life

Think of your mind like an exclusive club. Not everyone gets VIP access, and some people only get to stay in the lobby. Create access levels for the people in your life based on their impact on your peace. Level 1: VIP access for those who uplift, support, and genuinely make you feel good. Level 2: Limited access for people who are generally okay but sometimes a bit draining. Level 3: Lobby-only access for people who bring drama, stress, or toxicity.

These levels help you decide how much time and energy you're willing to give each person. The VIPs get more of your time and attention, while the lobby-dwellers get limited interaction. This mental framework lets you protect your peace by filtering who gets close to you. Not everyone deserves full access to your life, and that's perfectly okay.

4. Practice the "Unfollow and Unfriend" Ritual

This might sound trivial, but it's a game-changer. Social media is a breeding ground for drama, judgment, and negativity. If you're serious about protecting your peace, start unfollowing or muting anyone whose posts disrupt your mental space. You don't need to see every rant, every complaint, or every unsolicited opinion that pops up on your feed.

Go through your friends list and unfollow anyone who brings negativity into your space. If that feels too harsh, at least mute them so they're not cluttering your mind. Social media should be a place that uplifts you or, at the very least, doesn't stress you out. Protect your peace by curating your online world just as carefully as your real one.

Guarding Your Peace Like a Fortress

Here's the bottom line: your peace is priceless. It's the foundation of your happiness, your focus, and your sanity. But in a world full of drama, gossip, and judgment, that peace is constantly under threat. Protecting it isn't just a nice idea; it's a necessity. Whether you're gently distancing yourself from negativity or going all-in and cutting ties with toxic people, remember that protecting your peace is your right.

So start with the small steps if you need to—politely pivot out of gossip, set a few gentle boundaries, and practice keeping drama at a distance. And if you're ready to go all-out, cut off the energy vampires, establish firm boundaries without apologies, and give access only to those who uplift you.

Your inner peace isn't something you owe to anyone else. It's yours to protect, yours to nurture, and yours to enjoy. So stand firm, protect your peace, and don't let anyone disrupt the calm you've worked so hard to create.

PROTECTING YOUR INNER PEACE TO-DO

Exercises:

1. **Set a Boundary and Stick to It:** *Identify one situation or relationship where you need a boundary. Set it and enforce it. Notice how it feels to protect your peace actively.*

2. **Create a "Peace Plan":** *Make a list of things or people that regularly disturb your peace. Decide on one action you can take to limit their influence on your life.*

Journal Prompts:

- *"What am I allowing into my life that disrupts my peace, and why am I allowing it?"*

- *"What would a truly peaceful day look like for me, and how can I work toward it?"*

CHAPTER 8
RADICAL SELF

"You are enough, right now, without changing a damn thing."

Alright, it's time to talk about the big one: self-acceptance. Real, radical, unfiltered self-acceptance. The kind that lets you walk through the world without needing everyone else's approval to feel good about yourself. Sounds nice, right? But let's get real—most of us are *terrible* at it. We spend so much time twisting ourselves to fit what we think other people want, adapting our personalities, hiding our quirks, and even changing our beliefs just to keep everyone else comfortable. And for what? For a fleeting moment of validation? A crumb of approval?

Practicing radical self-acceptance is about flipping that script completely. It's about taking a good, hard look at who you are, flaws and all, and deciding that you're pretty damn awesome exactly as you are. It's about reducing your dependency on others' opinions, learning to stop measuring yourself by someone else's ruler, and finally becoming *your own* biggest fan. Sound intimidating? Don't worry; we'll ease into it. We'll start with the light approach for those who are just dipping their toes in the waters of self-acceptance, and then we'll dive into the deep end with a full-on "zero tolerance" policy for self-criticism.

Why Radical Self-Acceptance Matters

Here's the harsh truth: if you don't accept yourself, you're going to spend your entire life waiting for everyone else to do it for you. And let's be honest: other people are way too busy worrying about themselves to constantly validate you. If you keep chasing approval from others, you're going to end up exhausted, frustrated, and constantly feeling "not good enough." Radical self-acceptance is your way out of that cycle. It's about choosing to love yourself fiercely, unconditionally, and without apologies. When you do that, you stop needing everyone else's approval. You become your own source of validation, your own biggest fan, and your own best friend.

The Light Approach

If you're not quite ready to declare yourself the President of Your Own Fan Club, that's okay. Radical self-acceptance doesn't happen overnight, and you don't have to go from zero to hero in one go. This light approach is all about practicing small acts of self-kindness that add up over time. Think of it as planting seeds of self-acceptance, one little gesture at a time.

1. Talk to Yourself Like You'd Talk to a Friend

Here's a simple question: would you ever talk to your friends the way you talk to yourself? Probably not. You wouldn't call them stupid for making a mistake, or berate them for looking a little rough in the morning, or guilt-trip them for eating dessert. So why do we think it's okay to do that to ourselves?

The next time you catch yourself being harsh or critical, pause and imagine what you'd say if a friend came to you with the same issue. Chances are, you'd be supportive, kind, and understanding. You'd remind them that everyone makes mistakes and that they're still amazing, even on their worst days. Start practicing that same kindness with yourself. Talk to yourself like someone you genuinely care about.

2. Treat Yourself to Little Acts of Kindness

Self-kindness isn't just about the big gestures; sometimes, it's the little things that remind you that you're worth the effort. Treat yourself to something you love, just because you can. Buy yourself flowers, take yourself out for coffee, or give yourself permission to spend an entire day doing absolutely nothing productive. These small acts of kindness send a powerful message: *I am worthy of love and care, even from myself.*

Self-kindness is a habit, and the more you practice it, the more natural it becomes. Start with one small act each day, something that says, "I see you, I appreciate you, and you deserve good things." These moments might seem trivial, but they're building blocks of a self-acceptance foundation that will only get stronger with time.

3. Keep a "Compliments Journal"

This might sound cheesy, but bear with me. Start keeping a journal where you write down compliments, good things people say about you, or even things you notice about yourself that you like. It doesn't have to be anything major. Maybe someone said you were funny, or you felt great in a new outfit, or you managed to stay calm in a stressful situation. Write it down.

Over time, this journal will become a treasure trove of positivity—a reminder of all the good things about you that you might overlook on a bad day. It's a way to counterbalance that internal critic with actual evidence that, yes, you're awesome. Flip through it whenever you need a reminder that you're more than just your mistakes or flaws.

THE HEAVY APPROACH

Now, if you're ready to dive in headfirst, let's talk about the heavy approach: adopting a "zero tolerance" policy for self-criticism. This isn't about cutting back on the negative self-talk; this is about eliminating it entirely. Imagine if, from this moment forward, you refused to say a single bad thing about yourself, no matter what. Sound intense? It is. But this approach is for those who are done letting self-doubt and self-criticism have the last word. It's time to kick the inner critic to the curb and replace it with radical, unapologetic self-acceptance.

1. Catch, Challenge, and Replace Negative Thoughts

This is going to take practice, but it's a game-changer. Every time you catch yourself thinking something negative about yourself, challenge it. Ask yourself, *Is this thought actually true?* If the answer is "no" (which it usually is), replace it with something positive. For example, if you think, *I'm such an idiot for messing that up,* replace it with, *I'm human, and everyone makes mistakes. I'll learn and do better next time.*

Think of it as mental jiu-jitsu—you're taking that negative energy and flipping it into something that empowers you. This technique works because it stops the spiral of self-criticism before it starts.

The more you practice it, the more natural it will feel to be your own cheerleader instead of your own worst critic.

2. Embrace Your Flaws, Quirks, and All

Radical self-acceptance means embracing everything about yourself, even the stuff that might make you cringe. Are you a little awkward? Embrace it. Are you stubborn? Own it. Maybe you're not a morning person, or you laugh a little too loud, or you snort when you find something funny. So what? These quirks are what make you *you,* and that's something to be celebrated, not hidden away.

When you embrace your flaws, you rob them of their power over you. Instead of letting them be a source of shame, they become badges of authenticity. They're proof that you're not trying to be anyone but yourself. Remember, people are drawn to authenticity, not perfection. So wear your quirks like a badge of honor.

3. Make "I Am Enough" Your Mantra

This one's simple but powerful: start telling yourself, *I am enough.* Every day. Write it on a sticky note, make it your phone wallpaper, say it to yourself in the mirror. *I am enough.* Let that mantra sink in until it becomes second nature. When you accept that you're enough as you are, right now, you stop feeling the need to prove yourself. You stop seeking validation outside yourself, and you start living from a place of self-respect and contentment.

Radical self-acceptance isn't about arrogance or pretending you're perfect. It's about recognizing that you're already worthy, no improvements necessary. When you truly believe that you are enough, the opinions of others stop dictating your happiness. You become rooted in yourself, and no amount of external judgment can shake that.

RADICAL SELF-ACCEPTANCE IS NON-NEGOTIABLE

Here's the bottom line: practicing radical self-acceptance isn't just nice; it's necessary. It's the foundation for a life where you're not constantly at the mercy of others' opinions, where you don't crumble every time someone doesn't approve of you, and where you're genuinely at peace with who you are. Self-acceptance is your armor—it's what keeps you standing tall in a world that's always ready to criticize.

Start small if you need to. Practice little acts of self-kindness, keep a compliments journal, and make a point to talk to yourself like you would a friend. And if you're ready to go all in, adopt a zero-tolerance policy for self-criticism, embrace every quirk and flaw, and let "I am enough" become the mantra that guides your life.

Radical self-acceptance doesn't mean you'll never have a bad day, or that you won't occasionally doubt yourself. But it does mean that, at the end of the day, you'll always come back to yourself with kindness, respect, and an unshakeable sense of worth. Because once you learn to truly accept yourself, you're unstoppable. You're no longer living for anyone else's approval. You're living for *you,* and that's the kind of freedom that changes everything.

RADICAL SELF-ACCEPTANCE TO-DO

Exercises:

1. ***Self-Compassion Challenge:*** *For one week, every time you catch yourself thinking a negative thought about yourself, replace it with something positive. Practice saying, "I'm enough."*

2. **Create a Compliment Jar:** *Write down one positive thing about yourself every day for a week. At the end, read them back to yourself as a reminder of your own worth.*

Journal Prompts:

- *"What would it take for me to believe, truly, that I am enough as I am?"*
- *"In what ways have I been holding back from fully accepting myself?"*

CHAPTER 9
WHAT TRULY MATTERS

"You can't prioritize everything—decide what deserves your energy."

Alright, it's time to get real about what actually *matters* in your life. We're talking about the big stuff—the people, goals, and values that are genuinely worth your time and energy. Because here's the truth: most of us are out here handing out our f*cks like free samples at a grocery store, giving our time and energy to things that, deep down, don't actually mean anything to us. It's like watering fake plants—no matter how much effort you put in, nothing's ever going to grow.

So, let's cut the fluff. It's time to stop wasting your f*cks on things that don't align with who you really are and start focusing on what truly matters. This chapter is all about helping you figure out what those core values and priorities are, so you can start living a life that's actually meaningful, instead of one that's just "busy."

We'll start with a light approach to help you make small adjustments and slowly shift your focus toward your core values. And for those ready to go full throttle, we'll dive into the heavy approach of overhauling your life goals and clearing out the noise, so you're only investing in what truly matters.

Why Identifying What Matters is the Ultimate Life Hack

Imagine this: every time you give a f*ck about something, you're making an investment. And, like any good investor, you want a solid return. But most of us are out here blowing our mental currency on things that don't give us anything back—empty relationships, pointless obligations, social expectations that don't align with who we are. It's no wonder so many people feel drained and directionless. We're investing in things that don't serve us, and then wondering why we're exhausted.

When you get clear on what really matters, you start living with intention. You become more focused, more energized, and, honestly, way more satisfied because you're not wasting time on things that don't align with your true self. Knowing your core values isn't just some "self-help" fluff—it's the foundation for a life that actually feels like *yours*.

The Light Approach

Maybe you're not ready to flip your entire life upside down, and that's okay. Even small adjustments can make a big difference in helping you align your life with your core values. This light approach is all about making subtle shifts that gradually bring you closer to what really matters.

1. Figure Out Your Top 3 Core Values

If I asked you right now what your top three values are, could you answer without hesitation? Probably not—and that's okay. Most people haven't taken the time to think about what truly drives them. But if you're serious about mastering the art of selective f*ck-giving, you need to know what your core values are. Think of them as the GPS for your life. If you don't know what they are, you're basically driving around without a map.

Take some time to sit down and list out the values that genuinely resonate with you. Maybe it's freedom, creativity, growth, authenticity, connection—whatever feels true to you. Once you have your list, narrow it down to the top three. These are your non-negotiables, the things that should guide every decision, relationship, and goal in your life.

2. Do a "Daily Life Audit"

This one's simple: look at how you're spending your days and ask yourself, *Is this aligned with my core values?* Maybe one of your top values is "creativity," but you're spending most of your time doing mind-numbing tasks that make you feel like a robot. Or maybe "connection" is a core value, but you're barely spending any time with the people you love because you're drowning in work obligations.

Once you see the misalignment, make small adjustments. You don't have to quit your job or completely rearrange your life (yet). Just start finding ways to bring a little more of your core values into your daily routine. If creativity matters, carve out 15 minutes a day to do something creative. If connection matters, schedule regular time with the people who lift you up. These small changes add up, and they're a great way to start living more intentionally.

3. Say "No" to One Thing That Doesn't Align

Here's a challenge for you: say "no" to one thing this week that doesn't align with your core values. Maybe it's a social event that feels more like an obligation than a joy. Maybe it's a task at work that someone else could handle, or a favor someone asked you that doesn't really sit well with you.

The goal here isn't to become a "no" machine; it's to practice saying "no" to things that don't serve you, so you can make more room for things that do. Each time you say "no" to something that doesn't align with your values, you're making space for something that does. And that's how you start to live a life that feels *full* rather than just "busy."

THE HEAVY APPROACH

Now, if you're ready to go all-in on aligning your life with your core values, let's talk about the heavy approach. This is for those who are done with half-measures and ready to do a full-scale audit of their goals, priorities, and relationships. This approach requires courage, honesty, and a willingness to make some big changes. But if you're serious about living a life that's true to who you are, it's worth every uncomfortable step.

1. Do a "Life Goals Purge"

Take a long, hard look at your current life goals and ask yourself if they truly align with your core values. Are you pursuing a career that actually brings you fulfillment, or are you just doing it because it looks good on paper? Are you spending time with people who genuinely make you feel happy and supported, or are you just keeping them around because you've always been friends?

If any goal, obligation, or relationship doesn't align with your core values, it's time to consider letting it go. This doesn't mean you have to burn bridges or make drastic decisions right away. But start thinking about where you're investing your energy, and ask yourself if these things are bringing you closer to the life you want. If they're not, it's time to start letting go, little by little, until your life is filled only with things that truly matter.

2. Create a "Values-Based Bucket List"

Forget the typical bucket list filled with places to visit and daredevil stunts. Create a bucket list that's based entirely on your core values. If one of your values is "growth," put things on the list that challenge you and help you grow, like taking a new class, reading more, or learning a new skill. If "connection" is one of your values, make it a priority to deepen your relationships, plan memorable experiences with loved ones, and reach out to people who inspire you.

This values-based bucket list serves as a roadmap, showing you how to invest your time and energy in ways that truly align with who you are. It's a way of making sure that every goal you pursue is bringing you closer to the life you want, rather than just checking off boxes for the sake of it.

3. Embrace a "F*ck Yes or No" Mindset

This one's for the bold: from now on, everything in your life should be either a *"fck yes" or a "no." If something doesn't make you feel genuinely excited, aligned, and energized, it's a no. This applies to people, jobs, opportunities, events—everything. The "fck yes or no"* mindset is about removing the gray area, that space where we say "yes" to things we're lukewarm about because we're too polite, scared, or unsure to say "no."

When you start applying this mindset, you'll be surprised at how much mental space, time, and energy you free up. Suddenly, your life is filled only with things that genuinely bring you joy, fulfillment, or excitement. Imagine the power of living a life where every commitment, relationship, and goal is something you're genuinely excited about. That's the magic of "f*ck yes or no."

4. Build a Life That Reflects Your Core Values—Unapologetically

Once you've identified your core values and cleared out the noise, it's time to build a life that reflects them. This isn't about making small adjustments; this is about unapologetically aligning every part of your life with what matters most. It means choosing a career that fulfills you, surrounding yourself with people who respect and uplift you, and designing a daily routine that energizes you rather than drains you.

This might mean making some major changes. It might mean saying goodbye to people or things that have been part of your life for years. But every choice you make in alignment with your core values brings you one step closer to a life that feels *right.* A life where you're not just surviving, but actually thriving.

GET CLEAR, GET FOCUSED, GET REAL

At the end of the day, mastering the art of selective f*ck-giving is about living with purpose. It's about stripping away the superficial obligations and shallow goals, and replacing them with things that truly matter to you. Whether you're starting small by making daily adjustments or going all-in on a life overhaul, the goal is the same: to create a life that reflects who you are at your core.

Identify what matters. Align your life with those values. Say "no" to anything that doesn't serve your true self. Because once you know what you truly care about, you stop wasting your time on anything else. You start living for yourself, unapologetically, with a clarity and focus that changes everything.

So, get clear, get focused, and get real about what truly matters. Your time is precious, and your f*cks are limited—spend them wisely.

IDENTIFYING WHAT TRULY MATTERS TO-DO

Exercises:

1. *"Hell Yes" Inventory: Take an inventory of the past month's activities, people, and events. Make a list of what made you say, "Hell yes!" and what didn't. Use this as a guide for future choices.*

2. *Daily Values Check-In: At the end of each day for a week, ask yourself if you spent your time and energy on things that aligned with your values. Make adjustments as needed.*

Journal Prompts:

- *"What are my top three core values, and am I living in alignment with them?"*
- *"If I focused only on what matters most to me, what would my life look like?"*

"F*CK-FREE" LIFE BLUEPRINT

"Build a life that fits you, not what society says you should be."

Alright, so here we are at the grand finale: creating a *"Fck-Free"*
Life Blueprint. This is where everything we've talked about comes
together. All those selective "fcks" you've been guarding, the
boundaries you've built, the self-acceptance, the peace, the
clarity—this chapter is about putting it all into action. The goal? To
build a life where you only care about the things that truly matter to
you, and you leave the rest behind without a second thought. A life
that's intentional, meaningful, and—most importantly—f*ck-free.

Think of this chapter as your DIY blueprint for a life that's tailored
to your core values and priorities. We're going to walk through the
steps to build that life, from small daily changes to big, bold
moves. I'll throw in some exercises and reflections to help you
clarify what a "f*ck-free" life looks like for you and give you real-life
examples of what that can look like. Ready? Let's build.

Why a "F*ck-Free" Life Blueprint Matters

A "f*ck-free" life isn't about being apathetic or cold-hearted. It's not
about detaching from everything and everyone. It's about being
ruthless with what you care about, investing only in things that
align with your values and priorities. It's about stepping away from

meaningless obligations, from toxic relationships, from goals that don't make your heart beat a little faster. Because here's the truth: life is too short, your time is too valuable, and your energy is too precious to waste on things that don't genuinely matter to you.

Building a "f*ck-free" life isn't something that happens overnight. It's a process. But every step you take toward it brings you closer to a life that feels aligned, balanced, and—let's be honest—just plain satisfying. This blueprint is about designing a life where every choice, every relationship, and every goal feels intentional.

Step 1: Define Your "Hell Yes" List

The first step to building a "f*ck-free" life is getting crystal clear on what actually deserves your energy. Think of this as your "Hell Yes" list—the things, people, and goals that make you feel alive, excited, and aligned with who you truly are. If it doesn't make you say "hell yes," it probably doesn't belong in your life.

Exercise: Make Your "Hell Yes" List

Grab a pen and paper, and write down everything that you feel genuinely excited about. These are the things that light you up, the goals that make you feel fulfilled, and the relationships that bring you joy. Don't overthink it—just write down anything that makes you say, "Hell yes, this is what I want." Here are a few categories to get you started:

- **People:** Who brings you joy, supports you, and makes you feel seen?
- **Activities:** What hobbies, passions, or activities make you feel energized?
- **Goals:** What are the personal or professional goals that actually excite you?
- **Values:** What are the non-negotiable values that guide your life?

Once you have your list, keep it somewhere you can see it every day. This is your roadmap. If something doesn't align with your "Hell Yes" list, it's probably not worth your time.

Step 2: Identify Your "F*ck-Free" Boundaries

Now that you know what's important, it's time to get clear on what *isn't*. Building a "f*ck-free" life requires boundaries—firm, unapologetic boundaries that protect your energy and keep you focused on what actually matters. These boundaries are the walls that protect your "Hell Yes" list from the constant noise of other people's opinions, obligations, and expectations.

Exercise: Set Your "F*ck-Free" Boundaries

Take a moment to think about the things that drain you. These could be people, social obligations, habits, or even certain types of work that feel like a waste of your time. Write down at least three things that you're no longer willing to put up with. Here are some examples:

- **Social Boundaries:** No more saying "yes" to every invite out of guilt or FOMO. If it doesn't align with your values, it's a "no."

- **Work Boundaries:** No more taking on tasks that aren't your responsibility. Say goodbye to micromanaging and pointless meetings.

- **Personal Boundaries:** No more tolerating relationships that drain you. If someone's toxic, it's time to limit your interactions or cut them off entirely.

Boundaries aren't about shutting people out; they're about making sure that what you let into your life supports your values. These are the guidelines that keep you from spreading yourself too thin and ensure that every f*ck you give is an intentional choice.

Step 3: Design Your Daily "F*ck-Free" Routine

Living a *"fck-free"* life doesn't mean making big, dramatic changes every single day. Sometimes, it's about the small, everyday choices that add up over time. A *"fck-free"* routine is about integrating your values into your daily life in a way that feels manageable and sustainable.

Exercise: Create a "F*ck-Free" Daily Plan

Pick three small habits that align with your values and priorities, and commit to doing them every day. Here's what that could look like:

- **Morning Routine:** Start your day with something that aligns with your core values. If creativity is important, spend ten minutes journaling. If connection is important, send a quick text to someone you love. Make sure your day starts with something that *you* care about.

- **Midday Check-In:** Halfway through the day, pause and ask yourself, *Am I spending my time on things that matter to me?* This little check-in helps you course-correct if you're getting sucked into tasks or conversations that don't serve your goals.

- **Evening Reflection:** End your day by reflecting on one thing that brought you closer to your "Hell Yes" list. Maybe you said "no" to something that didn't align, or you spent time on a goal that matters to you. Acknowledge these wins to reinforce the habit of living intentionally.

These daily practices don't need to be huge, but they should be consistent. The more you integrate your values into your everyday routine, the easier it becomes to live a life that's authentically yours.

STEP 4: MAKE BOLD MOVES TOWARD A "F*CK-FREE" LIFE

Now, if you're ready to go all-in, it's time to make some big changes. A "f*ck-free" life isn't just about tweaking your schedule; sometimes, it requires major shifts that realign your life with what matters most. This might mean a career change, a relationship shift, or even moving somewhere new. Bold moves aren't easy, but they're necessary if you want to live fully on your own terms.

Identify One Bold Change

Think about one significant change you could make to bring your life more in line with your values. Maybe it's quitting a job that doesn't fulfill you, ending a toxic friendship, or moving to a city that feels more aligned with who you are. Write it down and sit with it.

Ask yourself: *What's one step I could take this month toward making this change?* Even a small step can set things in motion. Bold moves don't happen overnight, but once you start, you'll feel the momentum build. Living a "f*ck-free" life requires courage, but every brave choice brings you closer to a life that genuinely fulfills you.

Step 5: Regularly Revisit and Refine Your Blueprint

Your "f*ck-free" life isn't a static document; it's a living, breathing blueprint that will grow and evolve as you do. The things that matter to you today might not matter a year from now, and that's okay. The goal is to keep checking in with yourself, refining your goals, and adjusting your boundaries as needed.

Exercise: Quarterly "F*ck-Free" Review

Every three months, set aside some time to review your "f*ck-free" blueprint. Go back to your "Hell Yes" list, your boundaries, and your daily routine, and ask yourself:

- *Are these still aligned with who I am?*
- *Am I making progress toward the life I want?*
- *Is there anything I need to add, change, or remove?*

This quarterly check-in ensures that your blueprint evolves as you do. It's a reminder to stay focused on what truly matters, to keep making adjustments, and to continue building a life that reflects your authentic self.

REAL-LIFE EXAMPLES OF A "F*CK-FREE" LIFESTYLE

Need some inspiration? Here are a few examples of how small and big changes can create a "f*ck-free" life:

- **Small Change:** Decline social invites that feel like obligations. Use that time for something that truly aligns with your values, like a solo night in or working on a personal project.

- **Medium Change:** Restructure your workday to prioritize tasks that align with your goals. Block out time for projects that matter to you and delegate or say "no" to anything that doesn't.

- **Big Change:** If a job, relationship, or living situation doesn't support your values, consider making a major change. Apply for that job you actually want, distance yourself from toxic relationships, or move somewhere that aligns better with your priorities.

-

Crafting a Life That's Unapologetically Yours

At the end of the day, a "f*ck-free" life is about living with purpose, with intention, and with unapologetic clarity about what you want. It's not about fitting into anyone else's expectations; it's about building a life that feels *right* for you. A life where every choice, every relationship, and every goal aligns with who you truly are.

So, take this blueprint and make it yours. Define what matters, set your boundaries, build a routine that reflects your values, and don't be afraid to make bold moves toward a life that feels meaningful. Keep revisiting, refining, and realigning as you grow.

A "f*ck-free" life isn't perfect, but it's real. It's yours. And that, my friend, is worth every single step.

LIVING F*CK-FREE & PROUD

Congratulations, you've made it to the end of the journey—from caring way too much about things that don't matter to learning the art of selective f*cklessness. *If you've read this far, you're not just dipping a toe into the waters of not giving a f*ck*—you're ready to cannonball into the deep end. You're on the edge of a life where you call the shots, protect your peace, and live unapologetically for yourself. So let's take a moment to recognize the courage it takes to get here. You've put in the work, faced some uncomfortable truths, and learned to let go of a whole lot of nonsense.

But let's be real. This isn't a magic formula. You're not going to wake up tomorrow with a perfect, 100% "f*ck-free" life. Because here's the thing: change takes time. Sometimes you'll slip up and accidentally care a little too much. You'll find yourself worrying about someone's opinion, getting sucked into drama, or saying "yes" when you should have said "no." That's okay. This is a journey, not a destination. Progress isn't a straight line; it's more like a messy, winding path full of setbacks, detours, and learning curves. But every step you take is a step closer to a life that's truly yours.

THE JOURNEY FROM CARING TOO MUCH TO SELECTIVE F*CKLESSNESS

Think about where you started: worrying endlessly about what other people think, letting social pressures dictate your choices, handing out your f*cks to every random obligation that came along. Maybe you felt guilty for saying "no," or like you had to please everyone, or like your worth depended on the approval of others. It was exhausting. It was draining. And, let's be honest, it probably left you feeling like you were living someone else's life.

But look at you now. You've learned to stop handing out your f*cks like free samples at a grocery store. You've figured out what actually matters to you and started setting boundaries that protect your energy. You've made the choice to prioritize your values, to walk away from toxic people, to create a life that feels right on your own terms. That's no small feat.

Selective fcklessness isn't about caring less—it's about caring smarter. You're still investing your energy, but now you're only putting it toward things that bring you joy, purpose, and fulfillment. You're no longer wasting your time on people who drain you, goals that don't excite you, or expectations that don't align with who you are. You're choosing your fcks with intention, and that's the difference between a life that feels exhausting and one that feels genuinely meaningful.

Change Takes Time, and That's Okay

Let's be clear: none of this happens overnight. Building a "f*ck-free" life is a marathon, not a sprint. You're going to have days where you feel like you're totally nailing it—like you've finally cracked the code to not giving a damn. And then you're going to have days where someone's offhand comment worms its way into your brain, or you say "yes" to something you should have turned down, and you'll think, *Wait, I thought I was over this.*

Don't beat yourself up over the setbacks. That's part of the process. Real growth isn't about becoming perfectly f*ck-free all at once; it's about learning, evolving, and making gradual progress over time. Every time you choose your peace over drama, every time you say "no" to something that doesn't align with your values, every time you stand up for yourself, you're building that muscle. You're rewiring your mind to prioritize what actually matters to you. It's okay if it takes time. In fact, it should take time—anything worth doing usually does.

And here's a little secret: the more you practice selective f*cklessness, the more natural it becomes. Eventually, you'll find that protecting your peace and living by your own values becomes second nature. You'll start to make these choices effortlessly, because they feel right, because they align with who you really are.

LIVING UNAPOLOGETICALLY, FOR YOURSELF

Here's the bottom line: you get one life. One. That's it. And you deserve to live it in a way that makes you happy, fulfilled, and at peace. You don't owe anyone an explanation for who you are, what you want, or how you choose to spend your time. Your life is yours to shape, and no one else has the right to tell you how it should look.

Living unapologetically doesn't mean bulldozing through life without caring about anyone else. It means making decisions that respect your values, your goals, and your happiness. It's about standing firm in who you are, even when people don't get it, and even when they judge you for it. It's about saying, "This is who I am, and I'm okay with that," without feeling the need to explain or justify yourself to anyone.

So go ahead—live boldly, live proudly, live without shame or guilt. Be selective with your f*cks, and don't apologize for it. Set boundaries like they're going out of style, protect your peace like it's your most prized possession, and embrace every quirk, flaw, and unique part of yourself that makes you *you.*

Final Words of Wisdom for the F*ck-Free Life

As you step out into this new, more intentional way of living, remember a few key things:

- **You don't owe anyone your energy.** Choose where you invest it wisely.
- **Boundaries are a gift to yourself.** Set them without guilt.
- **Your value isn't tied to anyone else's opinion.** You're enough just as you are.
- **Embrace the messiness of growth.** This journey isn't always pretty, but it's worth it.

And finally, remember this: living a "f*ck-free" life isn't about shutting out the world. It's about finding what truly makes you happy, what brings you peace, and what aligns with your deepest values. It's about stripping away the noise, the nonsense, and the needless stress, so you can focus on the things that actually make your life meaningful. It's about freeing yourself to live boldly, authentically, and unapologetically.

So here's to you, living *fck-free and proud. Here's to a life that's intentional, joyful, and truly yours. Go out there and live it—one selective, intentional, unapologetic fck* at a time.

BONUS: BALANCE

Alright, here's the thing: not giving a f*ck *is liberating, but there's a fine line between freedom and delusion. If you're out here handing out zero f*cks like candy at a parade without a shred of self-reflection, you're going to end up living in a bubble of your own making. And newsflash: that bubble might feel invincible, but it can be just as dangerous as caring too much about what people think.

This chapter is about striking the balance between the liberating art of not giving a f*ck and the crucial skill of self-awareness. Because let's face it—sometimes, people's opinions and feedback actually contain a sliver (or more) of truth. And if you're so caught up in living a "f*ck-free" life that you never pause to ask, Could they have a point?, then you're missing out on some major opportunities for growth.*

Let's get one thing clear right off the bat: self-reflection isn't the enemy of living a f*ck-free life. In fact, it's one of the best tools you've got for keeping your life in alignment. Because the goal here isn't to be oblivious; it's to be intentional. You want to make sure that the "f*cks" you choose not to give are actually irrelevant and that you're not just brushing off valid points because it's easier than facing uncomfortable truths.

Why Self-Awareness is Your Best Friend

Here's the brutal truth: if you walk through life convinced that you're right about everything and that no one else has anything worthwhile to say, you're not just f*ck-free; you're closed off. And that's not empowering—that's just shortsighted. Being self-aware doesn't mean you're bending over backward to accommodate everyone's opinions. It just means you're taking a moment to check in with yourself, to make sure you're not missing something important.

Self-awareness is what keeps you grounded. It's what stops you from floating off into your own echo chamber where everyone (including you) thinks you're flawless. When you practice self-reflection, you're giving yourself the chance to grow, to get better, to realign with your values if you've accidentally drifted. And, most importantly, you're making sure that the people you do trust—the inner circle whose opinions you actually respect—have the chance to keep you accountable.

How to Balance Not Giving a F*ck with Self-Reflection

Let's break this down into a few actionable steps. This isn't about abandoning your hard-won sense of independence; it's about creating a little space for self-checks along the way. Because if you're going to live a life where you don't give a damn about unnecessary opinions, you'd better make sure you're rock-solid on what actually matters.

1. Listen, Don't Absorb

Here's a skill worth mastering: learning to listen without absorbing. When someone gives you feedback or shares an opinion, listen to it without immediately internalizing it. Think of it like window-shopping—you're looking, you're considering, but you're not buying.

When someone throws their two cents at you, take a mental step back and think, *Is this worth my energy?* If it's just noise, let it roll off. But if it's coming from someone you respect, someone who knows you well and cares about your growth, it might be worth a second look. Listen without taking it personally, and let the idea sit with you for a bit. You're still in control, but you're giving yourself the chance to learn without immediately shutting down.

2. Consult Your Inner Circle (A.K.A., The Trusted Few)

Everyone needs an inner circle—a handful of people whose opinions actually matter because they know you and have your back. These are the people who'll tell you the hard truths, who aren't afraid to call you out when you're off track, and who genuinely want to see you grow. When you're faced with feedback or criticism that leaves you questioning, take it to your inner circle.

Run it by them: *Hey, do you think there's any truth to this? Am I missing something here?* Sometimes, they'll confirm that the feedback is nonsense and that you're better off ignoring it. Other times, they might give you a gentle nudge and say, "Actually… they kind of have a point." Either way, you're not blindly dismissing things that could actually help you grow. You're filtering it through the people who genuinely want what's best for you.

3. Do a Brutal Honesty Self-Check

Now, this part isn't easy, but it's crucial. Every once in a while, you need to have a brutally honest check-in with yourself. No excuses, no justifications—just a moment to ask, *Am I truly living in alignment with my values?* This self-check isn't about beating yourself up; it's about keeping yourself accountable.

When you do this, be ready to face the good, the bad, and the ugly. Are there areas where you've gotten lazy or let your standards slip? Are you holding onto certain behaviors or beliefs that don't serve you anymore? Are you brushing off valid criticisms because they're uncomfortable? Be real with yourself. The goal here is to make sure you're living in line with your principles, not just doing whatever's easiest in the name of "not giving a f*ck."

4. Separate Feedback into "Useful" and "Useless" Piles

Here's a little exercise for you. Every time you get feedback, mentally sort it into one of two piles: Useful or Useless. Useful feedback is anything that aligns with your values, comes from a trusted source, or highlights something that actually deserves attention. Useless feedback is everything else—opinions from people who don't know you, critiques that don't align with your goals, and, of course, judgmental nonsense from randoms who don't matter.

The key here is to trust yourself to make the distinction. Don't let your ego throw everything into the "Useless" pile just because it's easier. Give each piece of feedback a fair evaluation, then toss it into the appropriate pile. If it's useful, act on it. If it's useless, let it go without a second thought. This practice keeps you open to growth while filtering out the garbage.

Embrace the Power of Moving On

Once you've done your self-reflection, consulted your inner circle, and sorted the feedback, it's time to let it go. If you've decided that the criticism is unwarranted, if you've done the work to make sure you're not missing anything, then move the f*ck on. Don't let it fester, don't keep picking at it, and don't waste another ounce of energy on it.

Moving on is a skill in itself. It's about trusting that you've done the work to evaluate the feedback, and now you're free to let it go. The beauty of self-awareness is that it allows you to learn, adjust, and grow without getting bogged down by other people's opinions. You've done your due diligence—now it's time to let it roll off your back.

Self-Awareness and Selective F*cklessness are a Power Combo

Here's the bottom line: self-awareness and selective *fcklessness* *aren't enemies; they're allies. Together, they help you live a life that's both intentional and unburdened. Self-reflection keeps you grounded, makes sure you're not missing out on valuable growth, and keeps you honest. And selective fcklessness frees you from* wasting your energy on opinions that don't matter.

A life without self-awareness is just reckless, but a life without selective f*cklessness is exhausting. Balance the two, and you've got a recipe for true freedom. You're living in alignment, holding yourself accountable, and focusing on what actually matters—all without getting tangled in everyone else's opinions.

So go forth and live boldly. Listen, reflect, grow—but don't be afraid to move the *fck on when something isn't worth your time. Because in the end, a life that balances self-reflection with selective fcklessness* is a life that's intentional, empowered, and unapologetically yours.

BALANCE TO-DO

Exercises:

1. **Constructive Criticism Check:** Take one piece of recent feedback that's been nagging at you. Write down why

you're resisting it, and consult with a trusted friend to see if there's any truth to it.

2. **Weekly Self-Check:** Set aside ten minutes each week to ask yourself if you're living in line with your values and if you're ignoring anything important. Write down any adjustments you'd like to make.

Journal Prompts:

- "Am I genuinely living in line with my values, or am I avoiding self-reflection out of fear?

BONUS 2: ARE YOU LYING TO YOURSELF?

So, you think you're living a fck-free life. You've read the chapters, you've adopted the language, you're all about "doing you." But let's get real—there's a big difference between thinking you don't give a fck and actually living that way. Too many people talk the talk without walking the walk, convincing themselves they're free from all the noise when really, they're just repressing their feelings or ignoring what's actually bothering them.

This chapter is about facing a hard truth: a lot of people think they've mastered the art of selective fcklessness, but deep down, they're miserable. They're sad, they're stressed, and they're haunted by a creeping sense of unfulfilled potential because they haven't learned to truly let go. Living a fck-free life the wrong way doesn't make you "liberated"—it makes you numb, disconnected, and often leaves you feeling emptier than before.

THE DIFFERENCE BETWEEN "PRETEND" AND "REAL" F*CKLESSNESS

Let's break this down, because pretend fcklessness and real fcklessness are two very different beasts.

1. **Pretend F*cklessness** is when you say you don't care, but you're actually just suppressing your feelings. You're still secretly obsessing over what people think, but you tell

yourself you don't so you can avoid facing those uncomfortable emotions. People living this way may put up a strong front, but inside, they're constantly wrestling with self-doubt, shame, or worry.

2. **Real F*cklessness**, on the other hand, isn't about *ignoring* the opinions of others or pretending you don't care—it's about actively choosing where to invest your time and energy. People who are *truly fck-free don't spend time convincing themselves they don't care; they're so aligned with what actually matters to them that the opinions that don't matter barely register. Real fcklessness* comes from a place of confidence, clarity, and self-respect.

THE RED FLAGS: HOW TO TELL IF YOU'RE FAKING A F*CK-FREE LIFE

If you're wondering whether you're truly living a f*ck-free life or just wearing it like a mask, here are a few telltale signs you're still holding on more than you'd like to admit.

1. You Say "I Don't Care" Way Too Often

If you find yourself constantly saying, "I don't care," "Whatever," or "It doesn't matter to me," guess what? It probably *does* matter.

The louder you have to shout about not caring, the more likely it is that you actually do. Real *fck-free living is quiet. It's peaceful. People who truly don't give a f*ck don't have to broadcast it—they're too busy doing what they love and moving forward with what actually matters to them.

2. You're Secretly Obsessed with "Proving" How Free You Are

Here's another dead giveaway: if you're always trying to prove how little you care, whether that's through rebellious decisions, controversial posts, or constant reminders to others that "you're over it," you're probably not as free as you think. Real freedom doesn't need to prove itself. It just *is.*

If you're stuck in a cycle of trying to convince yourself or others that you're carefree, you're still tethered to other people's opinions. Instead of asking, *How can I show everyone I don't care?*, ask, *Why do I need anyone to know that I don't care?*

3. You Feel a Constant Low-Level Sadness or Anxiety

Pretending not to give a f*ck *can actually make you feel worse. If you're burying emotions and plastering a "fck-free" mask over the* top, those feelings will find a way to creep out. Living a life that's truly aligned with your values feels uplifting, freeing, and calming.

If you're feeling low, anxious, or disconnected, it might be because you're repressing genuine feelings rather than addressing them.

Ask yourself: *Am I really okay with this situation, or am I just telling myself I am?* If you feel a pang of sadness or anxiety, that's a red flag you might be ignoring something important.

4. You're Constantly on Edge or Defensive

A huge sign that you're not as free as you think? Feeling defensive every time someone questions you or calls you out. If you snap back or feel offended every time someone offers feedback, it's likely you're still holding onto their opinions, whether you want to admit it or not. People who truly don't give a f*ck don't feel the need to argue with every critic—they're too rooted in their own truth to be easily shaken.

HOW TO ACTUALLY LIVE A F*CK-FREE LIFE (WITHOUT LYING TO YOURSELF)

If you've recognized some of these signs in yourself, don't panic. This doesn't mean you're destined to live in self-delusion forever. It just means you need to make a few shifts to genuinely live with freedom and clarity, rather than just pretending you do.

1. Face Your Feelings Head-On

The first step to true freedom is facing your emotions. Ignoring them won't make them disappear. When something gets under your skin or you feel that creeping doubt or shame, take a moment to really sit with it. Ask yourself, *Why does this bother me? What am I afraid of here?*

Self-reflection is your best friend on the journey to a truly f*ck-free life. By facing your emotions, you get to the root of the issue instead of slapping a "don't care" sticker over it.

2. Focus on Alignment, Not Avoidance

Real f*cklessness isn't about running away from things that make you uncomfortable; it's about running *toward* the things that truly resonate with you. If you're constantly trying to dodge difficult emotions, you're still letting them dictate your life. Instead, focus on moving toward goals, values, and relationships that genuinely light you up.

When you're in alignment with yourself, you won't have to convince yourself to not care about the noise around you—it'll just naturally fade into the background.

3. Develop a Practice of Self-Check-Ins

Schedule regular self-check-ins to make sure you're still living in alignment with what matters. This could be a weekly reflection, a monthly review, or a quarterly life audit. Take the time to ask yourself, *Am I staying true to my values? Am I genuinely okay with my choices, or am I just brushing things off to avoid discomfort?*

This practice will keep you honest with yourself. It's a way to ensure that you're not just cruising along pretending everything's fine while resentment or sadness builds up underneath.

4. Stop Trying to Prove Anything to Anyone

Here's a simple truth: the less you need to prove your freedom, the freer you actually are. Real liberation doesn't need a stage or an audience. It's a private, internal thing, one that doesn't require validation from anyone else. Ask yourself, *Who am I trying to impress, and why?* If you can let go of the need to prove anything to anyone, you'll find that living authentically becomes a whole lot easier.

Real Freedom Feels Like Peace, Not Like Chaos

Living a truly f*ck-free life doesn't feel like shouting from the rooftops. It feels like peace, like calm, like clarity. It's about waking up in the morning and knowing that the only person whose approval matters is your own. It's about making choices because they align with your values, not because they'll make someone else envious or impressed.

If your "f*ck-free" life feels like an exhausting performance, it's time to rethink it. Real freedom is about understanding yourself, accepting the good and the bad, and moving forward with purpose. It's about living fully, but without the pressure to be anything other than who you are.

True F*cklessness Starts Within

So, here's the real takeaway: if you want to live a genuinely *fck-free life, start by looking inward. Stop trying to convince yourself or others that you don't care—just do the work to be at peace with who you are. Take time for self-reflection, face the hard truths, and remember that not giving a fck is an internal state, not* a performance for others to see.

Because the ultimate goal isn't to go through life unaffected—it's to go through life unaffected by the things that don't matter. When you achieve that, you'll know you've crossed the line from pretending to be free to actually living it. And trust me, there's nothing more powerful than a life built on real, honest, unapologetic freedom.

YOU'RE A F*CK-FREE WARRIOR

Alright, let's get one thing straight—you didn't just casually breeze through this book and pick up a few tips. Nope. You, my friend, went on a full-blown, soul-searching, f*ck-free journey. You slogged through brutal truths, stared down your inner people-pleaser, and probably questioned half of your life choices along the way. And yet, here you are, standing tall at the end of it all, possibly a little bruised but ten times stronger.

So before you strut off to conquer the world, it's time to give yourself some credit. Acknowledge what you just put yourself through. Because honestly? Most people wouldn't have the guts. Most people would take a look at a book on giving fewer f*cks, laugh nervously, and then go right back to stressing over their ex's opinions on social media. But not you. You signed up for the real deal.

YOU COULD HAVE SKIPPED ALL THIS—BUT YOU DIDN'T

Let's be real—living a f*ck-free life isn't exactly the easy way out. The easy way would be to keep caring about every little thing, to keep bending over backward for approval, and to let other people run your life while you lie there wondering why you're so damn tired. But you didn't choose that. Nope. You signed up to face the messy, uncomfortable truth about where you're wasting your energy and who you're letting drain it. You've gone head-to-head with your own doubts, your own insecurities, and all the stuff you used to let control you.

And that, my friend, takes a special kind of bravery (and maybe a touch of masochism). You faced all that, and you came out the other side. That's some next-level self-care. So yeah, take a minute to appreciate the hell out of yourself.

You Learned the Difference Between Pretending and Actually Not Giving a F*ck

Let's talk about this: there are plenty of people out there who think they're living a f*ck-free life because they walk around saying "I don't care" like it's a catchphrase. But here's the difference—you didn't just slap on a fake sense of freedom. You dug in deep and figured out what actually matters to you and what's worth absolutely zero of your time. You know the difference between a life that's genuinely free and one that's just performative apathy.

You didn't just act cool—you *became* cool, with your quiet confidence and your unshakeable sense of self. So go ahead and thank yourself for having the courage to do it for real, not just for show.

You Put Yourself First, and Yeah, That's a Big Deal

Society loves to sell the idea of putting yourself last—self-sacrifice, endless hustle, bending over backward to make sure everyone else is comfortable. But you? You flipped the script. You looked at your own needs, your own peace, and your own happiness, and you decided those things are non-negotiable. And guess what? That doesn't make you selfish. It makes you *smart.*

Thank yourself for that bold move because people will try to make you feel guilty about it. But you know better. You know that taking care of yourself is the foundation of everything else. You can't give from an empty cup, and now, you don't have to. Because you've got your priorities in order, and you're done apologizing for it.

You Did the Hard Stuff Without the Applause

Here's the kicker: no one's giving you a trophy for this. No one's lining up to congratulate you on finally giving yourself permission to live life on your terms. Why? Because they're too busy dealing with their own f*ck-giving crises. But here's the brutal truth—you don't need their applause. You don't need anyone's validation. Because you've figured out the ultimate power move: validating yourself.

You chose a path that doesn't come with likes or followers or constant approval from others. And that's what makes it real. So, give yourself a standing ovation because, unlike most people, you did the hard work even when no one was watching.

You're Done With the Bullsh*t—and You're Better for It

Think back to where you started: stressing about what everyone thought, giving your precious energy to people who didn't deserve it, constantly feeling drained and unfulfilled. Look at you now. You've leveled up. You know what matters, and you know what doesn't. You've mastered the art of saying "no" without guilt, you've established boundaries that would make Fort Knox jealous, and you've finally prioritized your own damn happiness.

You're not just "trying" to live a better life—you're actively *doing* it. And yeah, it's probably ruffled a few feathers along the way, but that's just proof that you're no longer bending to fit someone else's mold. You're free, you're fierce, and you're done with the bullsh*t.

THANK YOURSELF FOR CHOOSING YOU

Look, at the end of the day, you're the only person who's guaranteed to be with you from start to finish. So thank yourself for putting in the work, for showing up for yourself when it mattered, and for not giving up on creating a life that feels good to you. No one else did this. *You* did this. You made this happen, and you're the one who gets to enjoy the benefits.

So go ahead, raise a glass, give yourself a fist bump, or whatever floats your boat, because you've earned it. You've put yourself first in a world that constantly tells you not to, and that's a damn powerful thing.

WHAT'S NEXT? KEEP OWNING IT.

So, what's next? Keep owning this life you've built. Keep showing up for yourself every single day. Keep setting boundaries, keep prioritizing your peace, and keep being unapologetically true to yourself. You've got all the tools now, and you've proven that you're more than capable of living a life that's actually worth living.

Because in the end, a life well-lived is one where you don't have to fake anything, especially not freedom. And you? You're living it for real.

So thank yourself, walk out that door, and go live your life like the absolute badass you are. No go be f*ck FREE!

WHY CHECK OUT MORE OF OUR BOOKS?

(LIKE, RIGHT NOW)

Alright, so you made it through this book, huh? Well, guess what? We've got a whole library of other books waiting for you, and if you thought this one was good, just wait. Inked Crown Publishing isn't just here to slap together some "meh" reads for you to toss on the coffee table. No, no, no—we're all about giving you the kind of books you actually want to pick up. From laugh-out-loud stories to tear-jerkers, high-res photography books that practically jump off the page, coloring books to chill with, journals for all your messy thoughts, and guides that actually help you level up your life, we've got the goods.

Here's the deal: if you've read this far, then you know we're not here to waste your time with bland, cookie-cutter content. We're the publishing house that *gets it*. We're here for the readers who want books with a personality—a little humor, a little grit, and a whole lot of heart.

Search Inked Crown Publishing on Google or Amazon today!

Disclaimer

This book is not for the faint of heart, the perpetually offended, or anyone who insists on taking life too seriously. It's also not a substitute for professional advice, mental health guidance, or the wisdom of a licensed therapist. If you're dealing with any serious issues that require help beyond what a book can offer, please reach out to a qualified professional.

Fair warning: This book contains sarcasm, blunt language, brutal honesty, and potentially some ideas that may challenge your current way of thinking. The concepts within are designed to help readers rethink where they place their energy, but remember: what you do with this advice is entirely up to you. You are responsible for your own choices, and we're not liable if a newfound "f*ck-free" attitude leads to any unexpected life changes, confrontations, or sudden clarity about things you don't actually want to be doing.

So, read with an open mind, a sense of humor, and maybe a pinch of salt. If you're easily offended or allergic to personal growth, consider this your cue to close the book. For everyone else, welcome aboard, and get ready for a dose of unapologetic self-reflection.

Disclaimer over. Now go give fewer f*cks responsibly.

F*CK YES F*CK NO

THE NO F*CKS GIVEN GUIDE TO SAYING NO, SETTING BOUNDARIES, AND LIVING LIFE ON YOUR TERMS

For the ones who are done with overthinking and pleasing everyone but themselves—this book is your brutally honest guide to saying yes to what matters and no to what doesn't.